Experts Sports Quiz Book

by
George L. Flynn

Distributed by
LOUIS J. MARTIN & ASSOCIATES, INC.
New York, N.Y.
Distributors to the trade

Acknowledgement: The author wishes to thank John Garrett of Schenley Industries who suggested the idea for this book. Thanks also go to Cliff Kachline of the Baseball Hall of Fame and Joe Horrigan of the Football Hall of Fame for their help in supplying pictures for the book. And to Bill Dippel who took a very tight schedule and a late manuscript and brought everything together.

Cover Illustration: Ted Burwell

First printing, June, 1979
Second printing, September, 1979

The "Experts" Sports Quiz Book
Published by Ramapo Media, Inc.
Oakland, N.J. 07436
All rights reserved
Printed in the U.S.A.

ISBN 0-916800-23-7

Distributed by
Louis J. Martin & Associates Inc.
95 Madison Ave.
New York, N.Y. 10016

Copyright 1979 by George L. Flynn

Dedication: To my wife, Jill, who over the years has sat through a lot of hours of sports watching without complaining.

Contents

1. Introduction 7
2. Baseball 14
3. "My Team Can Beat Your Team" 21
4. Nicknames 39
5. Football 47
6. Super Bowl 59
7. Picture Quiz 71
8. Basketball 107
9. Words, Rules and Signals 118
10. Who Am I? 126
11. Golf, Tennis, Horse Racing and Other Sports 149
12. Sports Goes to the Movies 158
13. Twenty Trivia Toughies 167
14. Epilog 178
    Picture Answers (except chapter 7) 191

Name this great football player and the position he played?

Chapter 1
Introduction

There is an old proverb that instructs us to refrain from discussions of religion or politics if we wish to get along with our fellow man. Good advice—as experience has proven. And conversations about one's operation, one's children or the latest book one has read or movie seen can also bore those listening. But let the topic be last week's football game, or the batting average of the local hero, or why that stupid coach doesn't play the player everyone agrees is the best, and friends or just brief acquaintances are all joining in and having a hell-of-a good time.

It almost never fails. Whether sitting on an airplane next to a stranger, or in the local pub, or at some cocktail party you didn't want to attend, just let the conversation begin with sports and soon, the stranger has a name and a smile, the cocktail party is fun, and the pub crackles with good fellowship and an extra round—sometimes even on the house.

There are few inhibitions about joining in the conversation. Perfect strangers will offer their opinions on some sports point and nobody takes offense. Sports is probably the best "ice-breaker" we have for making friends with newcomers into the neighborhood, and it certainly helps the new kid on the block if he is a good athlete. Even if he isn't but he knows his sports, he'll have an easier time getting accepted by the others.

America is a special place for sports, and the American is a one-of-a kind sports fan. Soccer is the big sport around the rest of the world. We have baseball, football, basketball, hockey, golf, tennis, swimming, horse racing and the rest vying for our attention and our dollars. Sure, they play tennis in other parts of the world but not like here. And there are golf courses too, but few play. Field hockey is big in India. Here, girls play it. Cricket is big in the British Empire—which isn't so big anymore—but try to get twenty people to watch a match here and they would all be asleep in ten minutes.

One of the reasons Americans have such a vast interest in so many sports is that almost all of us played one of them at one time or another, and we understand boxing very well because all of us had to at least once put down our school books and settle things. We grew up playing baseball or basketball, swimming and running, throwing a football or wrestling in the playground. Most of us never got beyond the competition level of the school intramural program, but we all participated in some sports. And when we watch the players of today, we can relate to what they are trying to do because we tried ourselves. If we were good enough to have made the high school varsity team in any sport, we consider ourselves experts in how that sport is played. Also, when remembering our achievements, the three points we scored when the team was so far ahead that we got to play, now has become thirty—and were we not all starters?

The players and the teams gave meaning to our lives, and happiness was finding out that Stan Musial went four-for-four against the Dodgers. Staying up late at night, after lights-out, with that old Zenith radio under the covers, listening to Red Barber do his "simulation" broadcast of the Dodgers playing the Phillies in Philadelphia was more thrilling than any movie. And talking about the game the next day at school, and being the only guy that heard Barber, gave one a sense of power and self-satisfaction that you would almost burst you were so happy.

Our sports heroes were demigods. Before television, the newspapers and the trading cards and Movietone news brought our heroes to us so we could see what they looked like. If you lived in the rural parts of America, the radio was your magic seat at the games. The broadcaster was as much a part of the team as the starting pitcher, and he told all the wonderful things our heroes did and what great guys they were; and what stars to grow up with. In baseball, there were the Yankees of Ruth and Gehrig and then DiMaggio and Dickey; there was the Gashouse Gang and then "The Man", Stan Musial, in St. Louis. Boston had Ted Williams, and Cleveland had baseball's greatest strikeout pitcher, Bob Feller. In football, the college game dominated. Pro football was just beginning to catch on, and it would be television that would make pro football the number one sport of the country after World War II. Basketball was getting headlines with the play of Hank Luisetti of Stanford; and fans filled Madison Square Garden to watch the collegians. The pros were just a way to break up the monotony of marathon dancing.

World War II did more than change the dynamics of the world. For the most part, sports went on a war-time footing; and after it was all over, sports became bigger than ever. People paid the unheard-of price of $100 for a ringside seat to watch Joe Louis defeat Billy Conn in 1946. And in 1947, baseball's color barrier came down when Jackie Robinson came to Brooklyn to star for the Dodgers. Now great black baseball players joined the major leagues, and names like Campanella, Mays and Irvin and Newcomb joined the Musials and Williams and Mantles as baseball superstars. College football picked up where it had been before the war, and the National Football League in 1950 made two moves that would eventually bring it to the place it holds today. They absorbed three teams from the All American Football Conference, and they began to televise their games. One of the teams was the Cleveland Browns, and a master coach named Paul Brown would build the first great dynasty of modern football.

Sports exploded in the '60s and '70s with new franchises in almost every major sport. Television revenues allowed the leagues to expand and soon sponsors were falling over each other to get their message across through sports. A tremendous young golfer named Arnold Palmer came on the scene and, suddenly, America had a new hero. People who wouldn't know a nine iron from a flat iron watch tv whenever Palmer played. Golf tournament purses skyrocketed, and in a single season golfers now earn in winnings what Hogan or Hagen earned in a lifetime.

If the money athletes earn today is astounding, what comes to us fans is even more unbelievable.

We see the World Series free, watch great football every Saturday and Sunday, see basketball played by super athletes, and attend the top tennis and golf tournaments around the world. When the Olympic Games are played, we have a front row seat—thanks to television. In fact, we see the Games better than any of the spectators who paid those usurious prices to attend in person. Instant replay and the expert analysts who work the events give us a far greater understanding of the techniques and skills of sports than you get sitting in the stadium.

The American sports fan is deluged with information about sports—from scoring percentages to batting averages to what a horse did the first quarter in. Magazines and newpapers cover the events and the players with a never-ending stream of insight and information. The exploits and deeds of our favorites are chronicled for us so that there is nothing we cannot find out about a player, a team or a league. More space in the daily newspapers is devoted to sports than any other single subject; and the weekends on television are filled with games and matches from all over the world.

With all this coverage of sports, it's no wonder that most fans consider themselves somewhat of an expert and certainly as knowledgeable as the next person about sports and the people and events that make up the texture of sports. The fan may not have actually seen Bobby Thompson's home run that beat the Dodgers, but he can tell you the name of the pitcher that Thompson hit the home run off, the base runners, the score at the time Thompson came to bat and when this all happened. He may not have been in Yankee Stadium when Roger Maris hit his 61st home run, but he saw it on television and read about it so many times that he can tell you the team the

Yankees were playing, who the pitcher was, and what pitch Maris hit, where the ball landed and what Mrs. Babe Ruth did.

This book is about sports facts and trivia. All fans know a lot about sports and the people and events that have a special niche in our memory because of their talents or the special happening that surrounded the event. Many never saw Ty Cobb play, but they remember his feats and have heard from the elders what a great player he was. So questions about Cobb should not prove too difficult. And so for other great players and coaches and managers and fighters.

In gathering the information for this book, the aim was always to entertain as well as challenge the reader. Asking sports questions is fun, if you don't try to make them too obscure. The reader should have a chance to answer the questions correctly and not be stuck on some point so trivial that only one-in-a-million could answer the question. Throughout the book there are many references, especially in the answers, that will lead to correct answers of other questions in the book. Most of the questions cover the major sports and events in those sports that were famous and are still remembered by today's fans. Some of the questions will require a fair degree of background in the sport. And background means a long time affinity for the sport as a fan, not a player—although many of the readers will have played most of the sports covered.

There is no score to be kept, and all that is hoped for is enjoyment in testing your knowledge of sports—and testing your friends' knowledge. Many of the people in this book are very familiar to you, but some will require some thought. Hints have been offered where it was felt there might be some confusion or help needed. Some questions are long, and nobody is expected to get all the parts correct or list all the names correctly. But you'll have a lot of fun trying to remember who was a charter member of the Pro Football Hall of Fame and recalling some of the great exploits of these people.

One of the great things about sports is that we not only enjoy the competition, but we can relive it in conversations with our friends. So here are some questions to recall the moments and persons that have made sports such an integral part of our lives.

Chapter 2
Baseball

No sport has a greater tradition of "trivia" than baseball. The "hot-stove-league" came from baseball. Years ago, when there was little interest in pro football, and basketball was considered a sport to be played by those not good enough to be baseball players, there wasn't much for the baseball fan to do after the season ended except to talk about his favorite team and players. And since the teams that made up major league baseball then were all east of the Mississippi, except St. Louis, and north of the Mason-Dixon line, except Washington, winter closed in fast after the World Series. So the baseball fans would gather at their favorite bar, or the local firehouse, or country store, get comfortable and discuss the past season, speculate on the season to come, and relive great moments in baseball.

The genesis of the term, "hot-stove-league" came from those meetings around the pot-bellied stoves across the country. Famed artist, Norman

Rockwell, captured the mood and intensity of the "hot-stove-league" in one of his great covers for the *Saturday Evening Post,* then the most popular magazine in the country. And the discussions sometimes got as hot as the stove, especially when the respective talents of a Ruth were compared to a Cobb or Walter Johnson to Lefty Grove. And these fans took great pride in their knowledge of the game, the rules, the records and the many small points that classify one as an expert in baseball. Many a dollar changed hands and many a friendship was strained until the local arbitrator produced the latest issue of the *Sporting News* to settle the points of discussion.

Today, baseball is nationwide, and television brings us very close to the players and the excitement of the games. Whether the players today are better than their predecessors is always a point of argument. The records set in the past have been, for the most part, broken by the players of today. Records are set to be surpassed. The player that set the record looses nothing when it is broken. Their standards were set in games just as competitive as today's and against players just as good.

So here are a few questions about some special records in baseball and the players and personalities that dominated the game.

1. There are a number of players that were named Rookie of the Year and later were named Most Valuable Player in their league. But only one player has ever been named Most Valuable, Rookie of the Year and winner of the Cy Young award. (Remember, the Cy Young award is for the best pitcher of the year.) Who is he?

2. This player is the only player to be named, by unanimous vote of the Baseball Writers of America,

as the Most Valuable Player in the National League. Who is he? And when did he win the MVP?

3. During a Monday Night Baseball game, broadcaster Howard Cosell said that Joe Morgan was the only player ever to win back-to-back Most Valuable Player awards. However, he was wrong. Can you name the others that have won back-to-back MVPs? Giving Cosell the benefit of the doubt, only one other National Leaguer has done it besides Joe Morgan. Who is he?

4. If Joe Morgan and the correct answer to question 3. are the only back-to-back winners of the MVP in the National League, who are the back-to-back winners in the American League? And if you really feel confident, give the years for each.

5. From 1949 through 1964, the New York Yankees won the American League pennant every year except two. Name the two teams that beat the Yankees in those years, the exact year each of those other AL teams won, and name the managers.

6. What is the name of the manager who has won more American League titles than any other manager in the history of the American League. Also, how many titles did he win?

7. If you answered question 6. correctly, name the manager that has won the second most American titles and how many?

8. This player is the only player to win an American League batting championship during the period that Ty Cobb won 12 out of 13 batting crowns. Who is he, and in what year did he break Cobb's string of batting titles?

9. This Hall of Famer holds the mark for the highest single season batting average in the history of baseball. Who is he, what was the average, and in what year did he set the record?

10. Baseball records have never been kept in the computer-like fashion of records we have today. But beginning in 1920, they did keep records of how many runs-batted-in a player delivered in a game, a season, and in the World Series. Since 1920, the RBI title has gone to many great hitters. But only once has it gone to two players where they each drove in *less* than 100 runs in a season. Who are these two players, and how many runs did they drive in?

11. Using 1920 as the cut-off point for what we'll call the "modern game" of baseball, what pitcher holds the record of the lowest earned run average for a single season? And in what year did he set that record?

12. The Rookie of the Year selection began for the American League in 1949. Only one American Leaguer since they began the award has been the unanimous choice of the voters (Baseball Writers of America). Who is he, when did he win the unanimous selection, and for whom did he play?

13. Everyone remembers the home run that Bobby Thompson hit off Ralph Branca to win the National League pennant for the New York Giants over the Brooklyn Dodgers. But can you name the pitcher that the Dodger manager replaced with Branca? And who was the manager?

14. The Cy Young award was started to recognize pitchers for their contribution to a winning performance. Many 20-game winners were by-passed for the MVP award because the voters felt that players who played everyday should get this award. So they began the Cy Young award for the best pitcher of the year in 1956. Between 1956 and 1966, one pitcher won it three times. Who was he? After that, they made it on a league basis.

15. Since 1956, counting both leagues from

1966, the winning pitcher of the Cy Young award has received all votes seven times. Can you name those pitchers that have been unanimous choices of the voters for the Cy Young award since 1956?

16. "The Iron Horse," Lou Gehrig, played first base for the New York Yankees from 1923 to 1939. Whom did Gehrig replace as first baseman for the Yankees and who replaced him?

17. This Hall of Famer holds the record for most consecutive seasons leading the major leagues in home runs. Who is he, how many consecutive years did he lead the majors, and what were those years?

18. This great pitcher holds the record for the most consecutive shut-out innings pitched. Who is he, how many innings of shut-out baseball did he pitch, and in what season?

19. Since 1931, both the National League and the American League have had a Most Valuable Player of the year named by the Baseball Writers of America. Since that beginning, many great players have been selected as the best in their respective leagues for the season. All positions played have been honored, from catcher to outfielder. What position has received the *fewest* Most Valuable Player awards?

20. Assuming your answer to question 19. is correct, name the players that won the MVP award at that position. And if you think you can, give the year each won and the team for whom each played.

Answers

1. Don Newcomb, Brooklyn Dodgers; Rookie of the Year—1949; MVP—1956; Cy Young award—1956.
2. Orlando Cepeda, St. Louis Cardinals, 1967.
3. Ernie Banks, Chicago Cubs, 1958, '59.
4. Jimmy Foxx, Philadelphia Athletics, 1932, '33;
   Hal Newhouser, Detroit, 1944, '45;
   Lawrence (Yogi) Berra, New York Yankees, 1954, '55;
   Mickey Mantle, New York Yankees, 1956, '57;
   Roger Maris, New York Yankees, 1960, '61.
5. Cleveland, 1954, Al Lopez.
   Chicago, 1959, Al Lopez.
6. Casey Stengel, 10 AL titles.
7. Connie Mack, Philadelphia Athletics, 9 titles.
8. Tris Speaker, Cleveland, 1916: hit .386.
9. Rogers Hornsby, St. Louis Cardinals, 1924: hit .424.
10. G. Kelley of the New York Giants and Rogers Hornsby of the St. Louis Cardinals both drove in 94 runs in 1920 and tied for the league RBI crown.
11. Bob Gibson, St. Louis (NL), 1968 ERA of 1.12
12. Carlton Fisk of the Boston Red Sox in 1972.
13. Ralph Branca replaced Don Newcomb and the Dodgers' manager was Charlie Dressen.
14. Sandy Koufax, Los Angeles Dodgers in 1963, '65 & '66.

15. Sandy Koufax, 1963, '65, '66;
    Dennis McLain, Det. 1968 and Bob Gibson, St. Louis, 1968;
    Steve Carlton, Philadelphia Phillies, 1972.
16. Lou Gehrig replaced Wally Pipp and "Babe" Dahlgren replaced Gehrig.
17. Ralph Kiner, Pittsburgh Pirates, 6 times, from 1947-52.
18. Don Drysdale, Los Angeles Dodger, 58 innings, in 1968.
19. Third Base and three from each league.
20. American League: Al Rosen, Cleveland, 1953;
    Brooks Robinson, Baltimore, 1964;
    Harmon Killebrew, Minnesota, 1969.
    National League: Bob Elliot, Boston Braves, 1947;
    Ken Boyer, St. Louis, 1964;
    Joe Torre, St. Louis, 1971.

Chapter 3
"My Team Can Beat Your Team"

If we all had an opportunity to pick our "dream" team, who would we pick? If the sport is baseball, all of us would have Babe Ruth in the outfield and Walter Johnson pitching. But what if someone had already picked Ruth and another had chosen Johnson, there are still a great many players left to pick to make up a "dream" team.

Here is a game that can be played with two, three, four or more players. The rules are very simple. As many players as there are, taking turns, each picks ten baseball players *but once a ballplayer is picked, he cannot be selected by any of the other players*.

Once all the players have filled their rosters, then each puts together the batting order for his team. It is here that the player will really show how much he knows about the game. With the quality of players selected, the difference will be between the teams that are put together for a special ability.

For instance, if the player believes in a power lineup, then he is committed to the big inning and the fact that hitting will dominate in the big game. If a player believes in pitching and defense, then his selections and batting order will reflect players that were outstanding in the field as well as hitting and also have speed on the base paths to emphasize a running team.

The selection of ballplayers can begin by any process the players want—flip a coin, choose a number or draw straws. Once the order of selection is established, then it continues until all the players have ten ballplayers. The players can select eight fielders and two pitchers. If a player wants to go with just one pitcher and pick another hitter, he can—but he runs the risk, when defending his team, that he'd be without relief help.

The mythical World Series seventh game will be played at Wrigley Field in Chicago. The game would be played in the afternoon with the weather being perfect, sunny, temperature in the low 70s and a slight breeze blowing in from center. The reason for Wrigley is that it is still one of the most beautiful ballparks in baseball; the dimensions of the playing field are fair to both left and right handed hitters. It is 351' down the line in left and right field; 368' in the power alleys of left-center and right-center; and 404' to dead center. Also, watching a baseball game in Wrigley Field is something special because the seats are so close to the field that all the spectators can be close to the players and the action.

So let us begin. Here are the ballplayers that have been selected for this game. However, if you have a favorite that is not listed, select him by all means. This list is *not* intended to be limited to our selection. These ballplayers are the ones that seem to be the choice of baseball experts, and almost all of them are in the Hall of Fame or soon will be. A brief biography of each player is provided to help the players recall some of the great feats of hitting and pitching by our ballplayers. So good luck and let's see whose team would be the winner. There is no way to determine in this book who would win, so the players will have to select one of their friends who is not playing to be the judge. (Good luck to the judge.)

Here are the baseball players selected for this All-Time All-Star final World Series game. They are listed as outfielders, infielders, catchers and pitchers. The players can put them at any position they want. Some of these great players played more than one position and were outstanding at both.

PITCHERS:

(1) Dean, Jerome "Dizzy"—one of the most colorful players in baseball history; great strikeout artist; won 30 games in one season; and had his arm not been injured, he might have been the greatest of all-time. Played with the St. Louis Cardinals.

(2) Drysdale, Don—holds the record for most consecutive shutout innings. Also, key clutch pitcher in World Series games for the Los Angeles Dodgers; very competitive; great strikeout pitcher.

(3) Feller, Bob—great strikeout pitcher with devastating curve. Possibly had the fastest fastball in baseball history; pitched 3 no-hitters.

(4) Ford, Whitey—"winningest" pitcher in World Series history. Great control; curve ball; good pickoff movement; won over 250 games.

(5) Gibson, Bob—Great pitcher for the St. Louis Cardinals. Big strikeout pitcher; holds record of 35 strikeouts in World Series; best E.R.A. in modern National League history.

(6) Grove, Robert "Lefty"—300 lifetime wins; great strikeout pitcher; won 25 games per season for seven seasons. Once fanned Babe Ruth, Lou Gehrig and Bob Meusel of the Yankees with nine pitches.

(7) Hubbell, Carl—the mealticket of the New York Giants in the '30s. A great southpaw, he once won 24 games in a row; and in an All Star game, struck out Babe Ruth, Lou Gehrig, Jimmy Foxx, Al Simmons and Joe Cronin in succession. In his career he won more than 250 games and is in the Hall of Fame.

(8) Johnson, Walter "The Big Train"— greatest strikeout pitcher in history; winner of over 400 games with a team that was almost always in the second division; charter Hall of Fame member; most lifetime strikeouts in baseball history.

(9) Koufax, Sandy—has pitched 4 no-hit games, including one perfect game. As a clutch pitcher, he has struck out more batters in one World Series than any other pitcher. Possessor of blazing speed and a great curve ball, he was the most feared pitcher in baseball in the early 1960s; a member of the Hall of Fame.

(10) Mathewson, Christy—Some experts consider him the greatest pitcher that ever lived. A great natural athlete and leader, he won 373 games lifetime including 37 in one season. He pitched 3 shutout games in the 1905 series, beating the great Philadelphia Athletics team of that day. Righthander and clutch pitcher.

(11) Seaver, Tom—3 time winner of the Cy Young award; 3 times led the National League in lowest E.R.A., plus over 200 hundred strikeouts for 10 straight seasons. Great control and fast ball. Sure bet for Hall of Fame. Righthander.

(12) Spahn, Warren—won over 300 games; 3 times lowest E.R.A. in National League; great curve, fast ball and control. He probably possesses the best pickoff move in pitching history. Inducted into the Hall of Fame first time eligible. Lefthander.

(13) Young, Denton "Cy"—Today's pitchers are given the award in his name when they have had a great season. He won more games than any pitcher in history. Pitched 3 no-hitters, one perfect game; great competitor. Big man with marvelous control. Right-hander.

There are so many others that could be listed; like Rube Waddell, Lefty Gomez, Early Wynn, Hal Newhouser, Robin Roberts, Allie Reynolds, and others. But these thirteen will suffice. If you have others you think you would like pitching for you, please select one of them as part of your pitching staff.

CATCHERS:

(1) Bench, Johnny—Like all great catchers, Bench combines great hitting with power, a superb throwing arm, and the ability to handle a pitching staff. Ranks with the best of all time in all around ability. Right-handed hitter.

(2) Berra, Lawrence "Yogi"—the greatest clutch hitter in World Series history. He has played in more games than any other and also has the most hits of all the players in the history of the series. A three-time American League MVP. Bats left.

(3) Campanella, Roy—the heart and inspiration of the great Brooklyn Dodger teams of the late 40s and 50s. Superb handler of pitchers; great throwing arm; power hitter with high average for a catcher; a three time MVP in the National League. Right-handed hitter.

(4) Cochrane, Mickey—one of the fiercest competitors to ever play baseball; for ten years the best catcher in the American League with the great Philadelphia Athletic teams of the late 1920s and the Detroit Tigers in the early 30s. A great athlete; fast and agile; could hit with power and average and an excellent baserunner.

(5) Dickey, Bill—first catcher to catch more than 100 games for 13 consecutive seasons; averaged well over .300 for 16 seasons. A cool, unruffled catcher; became a starter with the Yankees in 1929 and hit the game-winning home run to give the Yankees the World Series in 1943. Hall of Famer. Right-handed hitter.

The five listed above are a representative sample of the greatest catchers in baseball history. There are others that could be in this list. Roger Bresnahan, Walker Cooper, Gabby Hartnett and Ernie Lombardi could easily be included. Maybe there is another that is your particular favorite. If so, put him on your team.

INFIELDERS:

(1) Banks, Ernie—the greatest home run hitter of any player that played shortstop. An outstanding fielder with great range; twice MVP in the National League, back to back. Hall of Famer. Right-handed batter.

(2) Boyer, Ken—hard hitting, great fielding third baseman of the St. Louis Cardinals. Won the National League MVP. Right-handed hitter with excellent power.

(3) Boudreau, Lou—Hall of Fame shortstop; American League MVP; great fielder and leader of the Cleveland Indians to the World Series title in 1948.

(4) Collins, Eddie—considered by most experts to be one of the greatest second basemen to have ever played the game. A top hitter and great fielder; member of the Hall of Fame.

(5) Cronin, Joe—top hitting shortstop of the Ruth era; good fielder; player/manager at Washington, won World Series. In the Hall of Fame.

(6) Frisch, Frank—player/manager of the great St. Louis Cardinals Gashouse Gang. A great "money-player"; a fierce competitor; excellent fielder and clutch hitter; first MVP in National League; member of the Hall of Fame, second baseman. Right-handed hitter.

(7) Foxx, Jimmy—great home run hitter. Fine first baseman with the great Athletic teams of the 30s; twice MVP of the American League; hit 58 home runs in one season; member of the Hall of Fame. Right-handed batter.

(8) Gehrig, Lou—played more games than any player in history. Great hitter, fielder, leader. Hall of Famer; left-handed hitter. Holds record for American League highest RBI; over 400 home runs; great clutch hitter.

(9) Gehringer, Charles—one of the great second basemen of all time. Classic fielder, excellent hitter, leader, member of the Hall of Fame; right-handed hitter. Played for the Detroit Tigers. American League MVP 1937.

(10) Hodges, Gil—great fielder, power hitter, leader. Right-handed hitter. Member of the great Brooklyn Dodgers teams of the 1950s.

(11) Killebrew, Harmon—home run king of third basemen; over five hundred in his career. Good fielder. Played with Minnesota Twins; right-handed batter. American League MVP in 1969 when he led league in home runs and RBIs.

(12) Hornsby, Rogers—holds the record for the highest single-season batting average. Greatest right-handed hitter in baseball history; excellent second baseman. Seven times National League batting champion; Hall of Famer.

(13) Lajoie, Larry—considered by experts to be one of the all-time greatest players in baseball history. A second baseman of superb talent in the field and a great hitter. Three times led American League in batting, hitting .422 in 1901. Hall of Famer.

(14) Mathews, Eddie—Hall of Famer and also has hit over 500 home runs while playing third base or first base. An excellent fielder with a good arm, he twice led the National League in home runs. Left-handed batter.

(15) Greenberg, Hank—first baseman of the Detroit Tigers, once hit 58 home runs in a single season; first unanimous choice as American League MVP; lifetime batting average of .313, four times led American League in home runs and three time RBI leader. Excellent fielder. Right-handed hitter.

(16) Rizzuto, Phil—From 1941 until 1956, he was the defensive heart of the great Yankee teams that dominated baseball. As a shortstop, he had excellent range and handled the double play as well as any shortstop. Handled almost 300 chances without an error; American League MVP; tremendous bunter and "hit and run" man. Right-handed batter.

(17) Robinson, Brooks—might be the greatest fielding third baseman in baseball history. A fine hitter; player who came up with the big plays in the toughest games. American League MVP and led in RBIs one year.

(18) Robinson, Jackie—Hall of Famer; one of the best competitors in baseball history; Broke the color line; Rookie of the Year; National League

MVP; batting champion; great base stealer; fine fielder and could play second, third or first in the infield. Right-handed batter.

(19) Terry, Bill—Hall of Famer; hit .401 one season; great glove man; player/manager with the New York Giants in the 1930s. Combined hitting for average with power, Left-handed hitter.

(20) Traynor, Pie—hit over 300 for ten seasons but most consider him the best fielding third baseman in the history of the game in the pre World War II years. Hall of Famer.

(21) Wagner, Honus—According to the experts, he stands alone as the greatest shortstop that ever played the game, Eight time National League batting champion; superb base runner; powerful arm; he may be the greatest all-around player of all time. Hall of Famer, one of five initial inductees, Right-handed hitter,

(22) Wills, Maury—held single season base stealing record; fine shortstop, good hitter, great competitor,

(23) Carew, Rod—leading hitter in baseball today. Has a chance to be first that hits over .400 since Ted Williams. Excellent fielding first baseman with good power and top RBI man. American League MVP, seven times American League batting champion.

(24) Rose, Pete—has over 3000 hits; good fielder; great clutch performer; excellent base runner; best switch hitter in baseball today. Sure Hall of Famer when eligible.

There are so many other great infielders that could be part of this group and should be considered in selecting your team. Infielders like Red Rolfe, Stan Hack, Arky Vaughn, Vern Stephens, Nellie Fox and Willie McCovey should all be potential players on any all-time team. And there are others that are not listed. The 23 listed seem to adequately represent the best of modern baseball and some of the all-time greats from the past.

OUTFIELDERS:

(1) Aaron, Henry—All-time home run leader, fine fielder, base runner; life time .300 hitter; holds all-time record for most RBIs and most total bases. Right-handed hitter.

(2) Brock, Lou—greatest base stealer of all time; powerful hitter for high average; top outfielder. Left-handed hitter.

(3) Clemente, Roberto—lifetime .316 hitter; four times led National League; MVP in 1966; great defensive outfielder with Pittsburgh Pirates; Hall cf Famer, bats right handed.

(4) Cobb, Ty—holds more hitting records than any player in history. Also, greatest base stealer in history until Lou Brock broke his record. Hit over .300 for 23 seasons; charter member of the Hall of Fame.

(5) DiMaggio, Joe—lifetime average of .325; great outfielder; home run hitter; and holds record for most games consecutively hit—56. Hall of Famer and three time MVP in American League. Voted "greatest living baseball player."

(6) Heilmann, Harry—great outfielder with Detroit Tigers and Cincinnati Reds. Lifetime average of .342, once hit over .400; top outfielder with great throwing arm; Hall of Famer, right-handed hitter.

(7) Jackson, Reggie—top World Series performer. Home run hitter and RBI clutch hitter. 1973 MVP in American League and MVP in 1977 World Series. Left-handed hitter.

(8) Kaline, Al—lifetime .300 hitter; member of the 3000 hit club; great outfielder; fine base runner. Right-handed hitter with Detroit.

(9) Mantle, Mickey—lifetime average at .298; 536 home runs; over 1500 RBIs; holds almost all World Series slugging records; three-time MVP in American League; greatest power switch-hitter in baseball history, great fielder; baserunner for New York Yankees. Hall of Famer.

(10) Maris, Roger—holds the home run record for a single season. Back-to-back MVP in the American League; fine outfielder with great arm; excellent base runner; left-handed hitter.

(11) Mays, Willie—only Ty Cobb, Babe Ruth and Honus Wagner got a higher percentage of votes into the Hall of Fame than Mays. Over 600 home runs in career; great RBI hitter; maybe the finest outfielder of all time; great base runner and base stealer. Right-handed hitter.

(12) Ott, Mel—lifetime .300 hitter; over 500 home runs in career; fine fielder; six times led the National League in home runs. Hall of Famer; left-handed hitter.

(13) Medwick, Joe—lifetime .324 batting average. MVP in National League; three times led the National League in RBIs, once in home runs. Great base runner/fielder; holds league record for doubles. Hall of Famer.

(14) Musial, Stan—"The Man"; lifetime .331 batting average; over 450 home runs; holds National League record for most hits; three times MVP in National League, played as All Star in outfield and first base. Great speed, smart runner, great clutch hitter.

(15) Robinson, Frank—only player to ever win MVP in both leagues, twice in American League.

Lifetime .300 hitter. Led American League in home runs in 1966, also RBIs; fine outfielder and base runner. Right-handed hitter.

(16) Ruth, Babe—greatest slugger in baseball history. Maybe the best all around player that ever lived. Held World Series pitching records to go along with his hitting. Lifetime .342 average; over 700 home runs; over 2200 RBIs. Experts consider Ruth to have been an outstanding outfielder who never threw to the wrong base. Charter member of the Hall of Fame. Left-handed batter.

(17) Speaker, Tris—considered by many to be the greatest outfielder of all time. Over .344 lifetime batting average. Charter Hall of Famer. Batted over .400 and is the only batter to interrupt Ty Cobb's consecutive batting championships.

(18) Waner, Paul—called "Big Poison", played in the big leagues for 20 years and had a lifetime batting average of .333. Fine outfielder, great hit and run hitter, had good power. Hall of Famer.

(19) Williams, Ted—considered by many to be the greatest natural hitter of all time. Lifetime batting average of .344; six time American League batting champion; last batter to hit over .400; over 500 home runs; twice MVP. Experts claim that had he not missed five prime years in the service, Williams would have set all hitting and slugging records of merit. Hall of Famer.

(20) Yastrzemski, Carl—Triple crown winner; American League MVP; power hitter for high average, great outfielder and can also play first base. Smart player, born leader. Left-handed hitter.

There are many other outfielders that could be part of the twenty listed here. Wee Willie Keeler, Ralph Kiner, Monte Irvin, Hack Wilson, Charlie Keller, Lloyd Waner, Al Simmons or even Casey Stengel, who hit a lifetime .393 World Series average. Maybe there is another you may want to have in your outfield.

The baseball players listed are most of the greatest to have ever played the game. There are enough listed to make up eight teams. A few pages have been provided so that the players can list their selections and then make up their batting order. Because each player will have so many greats to work with in organizing his batting order, the little intangibles that go into making a winning team are almost as important as the batting averages or number of strikeouts the ballplayers have recorded. The ability of one of the ballplayers to hit behind the runner, make the sacrifice bunt at the right time, turn over a key double play or come up with the strikeout when you need it, is what will determine the difference between the teams the players put together.

There will be no decided winner in these mythical World Series games. All that will come will be the enjoyment of pitting one's knowledge of the game of baseball, both statistical and emotional, against the others. And, after all, isn't that what being arm-chair managers or bleacher experts is all about? The chance to prove that each one of us, given the players of our choice, "can beat your team, anytime."

On the following pages, there are places for you to select your players. After all the selections are made, you have, next to your selections, a batting order slate.

Player No. 1 _____
Selections: Batting Order:

1. _____   1. _____
2. _____   2. _____
3. _____   3. _____
4. _____   4. _____
5. _____   5. _____
6. _____   6. _____
7. _____   7. _____
8. _____   8. _____
9. _____   9. _____
10. _____   10. _____

Player No. 1 _____
Selections: Batting Order:

1. _____   1. _____
2. _____   2. _____
3. _____   3. _____
4. _____   4. _____
5. _____   5. _____
6. _____   6. _____
7. _____   7. _____
8. _____   8. _____
9. _____   9. _____
10. _____   10. _____

Player No. 1 _____
Selections: Batting Order:

1. _____   1. _____
2. _____   2. _____
3. _____   3. _____
4. _____   4. _____
5. _____   5. _____
6. _____   6. _____
7. _____   7. _____
8. _____   8. _____
9. _____   9. _____
10. _____   10. _____

Player No. 1 _____
Selections: Batting Order:

1. _____   1. _____
2. _____   2. _____
3. _____   3. _____
4. _____   4. _____
5. _____   5. _____
6. _____   6. _____
7. _____   7. _____
8. _____   8. _____
9. _____   9. _____
10. _____   10. _____

Player No. 1 _____
Selections: Batting Order:

1. _____   1. _____
2. _____   2. _____
3. _____   3. _____
4. _____   4. _____
5. _____   5. _____
6. _____   6. _____
7. _____   7. _____
8. _____   8. _____
9. _____   9. _____
10. _____   10. _____

Player No. 1 _____
Selections: Batting Order:

1. _____   1. _____
2. _____   2. _____
3. _____   3. _____
4. _____   4. _____
5. _____   5. _____
6. _____   6. _____
7. _____   7. _____
8. _____   8. _____
9. _____   9. _____
10. _____   10. _____

Player No. 1 _____
Selections: Batting Order:

1. _____   1. _____
2. _____   2. _____
3. _____   3. _____
4. _____   4. _____
5. _____   5. _____
6. _____   6. _____
7. _____   7. _____
8. _____   8. _____
9. _____   9. _____
10. _____   10. _____

Player No. 1 _____
Selections: Batting Order:

1. _____   1. _____
2. _____   2. _____
3. _____   3. _____
4. _____   4. _____
5. _____   5. _____
6. _____   6. _____
7. _____   7. _____
8. _____   8. _____
9. _____   9. _____
10. _____   10. _____

What is this famous person's name and his nickname?

Chapter 4
Nicknames

The dictionary defines the word nickname as "a descriptive name added to or replacing the actual name of a person, place or thing." Many of the most famous athletes in sports are more recognized by their nickname than their given name. Everybody knows who Babe Ruth was but how many remember who George Ruth was. Mention Dizzy Dean and fans quickly remember the colorful strikeout artist of the St. Louis Cardinals, but if you asked a knowledgeable fan who Jerome Dean was he'd probably have to pause and even ask for a hint. Through all sports, certain athletes and teams have been given nicknames that stuck with them throughout their careers and afterwards.

All of us have probably had a nickname at one time or another. If you played sports, you probably called someone "Lefty" or knew a towhead that was called "Whitey." And remember how frightened you'd get when you knew the other team had a guy called "Moose" or "Rocky." And a kid nicknamed "Bronco" gave the opposition a decided advantage, at least before the opening kickoff.

The famed comedian, Myron Cohen once did a very funny routine about nicknames in football, decrying the fact that today's players don't have the fearsome nicknames like the players of yesterday. Cohen asked how anyone could be afraid of a Milton Plum (former quarterback with the Cleveland Browns and Detroit Lions) or Yelberton Abraham Tittle? Where, he wondered, were the Bronco Nagurskis, the Johnny Bloods, the Bulldog Turners of today? Well, maybe the football players of today don't have the frightening nicknames of yesterday, but they sure are big enough to even scare Bronco or Bulldog.

Some of the most famous nicknames in sports came about because of some physical characteristic of the athlete or a famous event for which the athlete will always be associated. Eddie Arcaro was nicknamed "Banana nose" because of the prominence of his proboscis. Roy Riegle will forever be known as "Wrong Way Riegle" because he ran the wrong way in a Rose Bowl game to snatch defeat from the jaws of victory for his California team. And the initials O.J. gave O.J. Simpson his nickname, "Orange Juice", later shortened to "Juice."

Listed on the following pages are nicknames of athletes and teams that have been famous over the decades since Abner Doubleday invented baseball—if it was indeed he who started our national game. The questions are laid out in a matching quiz, familiar to all of us. There are thirty matching questions. A good sports fan should get most; an expert, all. Some of the nicknames are of teams or schools, as well as individuals.

Nickname Match	**Real Name**
1. Whiz Kids	(A) Horse Racing—Georgie Wolff, a great jockey who was killed in a spill. Golf—Ben Hogan whom the Scots nicknamed "The Wee Iceman" when he played in the British Open.
2. Double X	(B) Alan Ameche—Heisman Trophy winner from Wisconsin, great fullback with the Colts in the pros.
3. Million Dollar Backfield	(C) Paavo Nurmi—the great distance runner from Finland who starred in the Olympics in 1920, 1924, and 1928.
4. Splendid Splinter	(D) James J. Braddock—A stevedore on the New Jersey docks, he knocked out heavyweight champ Max Baer in 1935 to win the title.
5. Big Poison & Little Poison	(E) St. Louis Cardinals baseball team that played in the early 30s. Featured rough and ready players, led by Dizzy Dean and Pepper Martin.
6. The Meal Ticket	(F) Stanley Ketchel—Middleweight champ in 1908, murdered by girl friend.

7. The Vow Boys	(G) Tony Lema —golfer, who ordered champagne for the press after he won a tournament. Killed in plane crash at height of career.
8. The Toe	(H) Tony Galento—boxer, fought Joe Louis for title, colorful character who trained on beer and raw oysters.
9. The Golden Boy	(I) Hal Newhouser— pitcher, Detroit Tigers, twice American League MVP.
10. The Iron Horse	(J) Basketball—University of Illinois team in the early 40s that was one of the best college teams in the land.
11. Murderer's Row	(K) The Chicago Bears— nicknamed in the late 30s and early 40s when they dominated pro football.
12. Galloping Ghost	(L) Hugh McElhenny— one of the greatest running backs in football history, with Washington University and the San Francisco 49ers.
13. Prayin' Colonels	(M) Ted Williams—maybe baseball's greatest hitter. Played with the Boston Red Sox and was the last batter to hit over .400.
14. Manassa Mauler	(N) Mickey Walker— Middleweight champion in 1922.

15. Crazy Legs	(O) Lou Groza—the great field goal kicker of the Cleveland Browns.
16. The Horse	(P) Jimmy Foxx—super home run hitter, twice MVP in the American League.
17. The Iceman	(R) Backfield of the Chicago Cardinals in 1947 when they won the NFL title. They were Paul Christman, Charlie Trippi Pat Harder, and Elmer Angsman.
18. The King	(S) Stanford University's football team in the mid-30's that, as sophomores, vowed they would never lose to Southern Cal. They never did in their three years.
19. The Flying Finn	(T) Carl Hubbell—Hall of Fame pitcher who played with the New York Giants in the 1930s.
20. Champagne Tony	(U) Paul Hornung—Notre Dame great. Only Heisman Trophy winner to have played on a losing team. NFL star with the Green Bay Packers.
21. The Cinderella Man	(V) Lou Gehrig—the immortal New York Yankee who played more consecutive games than any player in baseball history.

22. Two Ton — (W) The name given to any great batting order where four or more can kill you. The most famous was Babe Ruth, Lou Gehrig, Earl Combs, and Tony Lazarri of the 1927 Yankees.

23. The Prince — (X) Jack Dempsey-one of the greatest heavyweight champions of all time.

24. The Michigan Assasin — (Y) Elroy Hirsh—All America running back at Wisconsin and pro Hall of Fame with Los Angeles Rams, as a great wide receiver.

25. The Toy Bulldog — (Z) Centre College from Kentucky that astounded college football with its victory over undefeated Harvard in 1921.

26. Monsters of the Midway — (a) Paul Waner and Lloyd Waner—both in Hall of Fame. Paul had lifetime average of .333 and Lloyd had .316.

27. Gashouse Gang — (b) Red Grange—the legendary running back of the Golden Age of Sports. Also in Pro Hall of Fame.

28. Night Train — (c) Tony Canadeo—college star at Gonzaga University and Hall of Famer with the Green Bay Packers in the '40s and early '50s.

29. Strangler (d) Ed Lewis—considered by most to be the greatest wrestler of all time.
30. The Grey Ghost of Gonzaga (e) Dick Lane—Hall of Fame defensive back from the Detroit Lions and Los Angeles Rams.

Nicknames—Answer Key

1. (J)	11. (W)	21. (D)
2. (P)	12. (b)	22. (H)
3. (R)	13. (Z)	23. (I)
4. (M)	14. (X)	24. (F)
5. (a)	15. (Y)	25. (N)
6. (T)	16. (B)	26. (K)
7. (S)	17. (A)	27. (E)
8. (O)	18. (L)	28. (e)
9. (U)	19. (C)	29. (d)
10. (V)	20. (G)	30. (c)

Chapter 5
Football

Historians dispute when the American version of football actually began. Popular belief has it that the first game was when Princeton played Rutgers in 1869. But what they played that day was actually a soccer game. Probably the first football game played was between Harvard and McGill University in Montreal. Then they played a version of Rugby called the Boston game, which meant the players could pick up the ball and run with it. Had football stayed the way they played it then, there never would have been a Super Bowl or Rose Bowl. Nobody would have shown up because they would have been bored to death.

In the history of football, the decade of the 1920's began the tremendous popularity that football enjoys today. The heroes were from the colleges and universities across the country and the country rocked in the fall to great football played in huge stadiums. The football players and teams that stood out in the Golden Age of Sports are some of the most storied in football history. Red Grange, the ``Galloping

Ghost" of Illinois who electrified the sports' world with his brilliant broken-field runs, once scoring four touchdowns in 17 minutes against a Michigan team that was considered the best in the country, was probably the single greatest draw in the history of football.

The most glamorous team of the day was Notre Dame; and their legendary coach, Knute Rockne, was one of the most respected men in America. His Notre Dame teams were populated by some of the finest players in the country, including the famed backfield of the "Four Horsemen." Ernie Nevers was leading "Pop" Warner's Stanford team to greatness, and Bennie Friedman was passing to Benny Oosterbaan at Michigan.

And while the college boys were enjoying the fame and adulation of the fans, another group of football players were scratching to make a living. They were called professionals, and their league was named the National Football League. The public greeted their appearance on the sports scene with a big yawn.

While the colleges were playing to full houses, and the press was making Saturday's heroes national names, the pros were lucky to make expenses on Sunday. So the pros turned to one player to give them respectability with the public. Immediately after playing his last game for Illinois, Red Grange signed with the Chicago Bears. To take advantage of Grange's fame, the Bears played 18 games in about a month, all across the country. Fans flocked to see Grange, and when he came to New York to play, over 73,000 customers paid to see the "Galloping Ghost." They also saw professional football; and even though the next two decades would be difficult, professional football had a foothold on public interest. Nobody watching the pros back then ever thought that foothold would become the stranglehold pro football has today on the sports' fan.

There have been many great players since Red Grange and many wonderful teams at both the college and professional level. We have been treated to unbelievable upsets, super performances by individuals and teams. Today's pro player is a major celebrity, and stars like Namath and Hornung make highly successful careers after their playing days.

Football coaches become demi-gods and develop a following that goes far beyond the teaching of Xs and Os. Before his untimely death, the legendary Vince Lombardi was consulted by leaders of business and government about national problems—not how to beat the Dallas Cowboys. Bear Bryant of Alabama is as successful in business as he is in producing national champions, and with the unbelievable coverage football gets on television and radio, former coaches and players bend our ears each weekend with their "expertise." No self-respecting ex-coach or quarterback is without at least one network to broadcast his "insights." Unlike old soldiers, old ballplayers fade into broadcasting.

The money paid for broadcasting rights for football is so huge that oldtimers wouldn't believe what their game has become. The income generated by the bowl games for the schools and conferences that participate can spell profit on their whole year's Athletic Department's operation. For professional football, television is the main reason for profit and popularity. And for the fans, these games bring us the game as never before viewed. With the electronic devices available today, we see the action, and then have it dissected four or five different ways so we can enjoy the artistry and technique of these fine players.

Since the time of Grange, football has grown to such a place in our sports society that the championship of professional football can be viewed by more people than any other event in history. The tradition, the pageantry, the excitement and color of football make it an ideal spectator sport as well as one that gives us constant action and violence. Over the years, many great players have passed before us and memorable games by the hundreds have been played. Football has a great and colorful tradition. The questions that follow reflect some of the more outstanding feats and great moments in football.

1. Grantland Rice immortalized the backfield of Knute Rockne's 1924 team when he dubbed them the "Four Horsemen." After what Notre Dame game did he write those lines, who were the players that made up that famous backfield, what was the nickname later given to the Notre Dame line, and who was the captain of that great team?

2. Name the charter members of the Professional Football Hall of Fame in Canton, Ohio.

3. In 1955, pro football established an award for the player selected as the Most Valuable Player for that season. The trophy is called the Jim Thorpe Trophy. Name the first winner of that award and which player has won it the most times, including the fact that since 1970 the award goes to one player from the AFC and one from the NFC.

4. When was the first Rose Bowl game played, what two teams participated and what was the final score?

5. The Outland Trophy is awarded each year since 1946 to the interior lineman selected as the best of that season. Name the first winner and at which school he played.

6. In 1937 the National Collegiate Athletic Association established statistics to give the fans and newspapers data on which player was the leading rusher, scorer, passer, and other categories. Name the players that led college football in 1937 in passing, rushing and scoring.

7. In the 1930s one of the greatest passing combinations in college football played for Alabama. Who was the passer, name the great end, and name the other end on that team that also won the Rose Bowl that year. Also, who did they beat in the Rose Bowl?

8. The first Super Bowl game created so much excitement because it was the first game between the warring leagues. Also, the fight was between the two networks that carried the different leagues; CBS representing the NFL and NBC carrying the games of the AFL. Commissioner Pete Rozelle ruled that because it would be unfair to eliminate one network, he decided to allow both networks to televise the game. Name the broadcasters for the two networks that covered Super Bowl I.

9. The Green Bay Packers of Vince Lombardi won 9 of 10 playoff and championship games. No record in football history matches that for clutch preformance when it counted. Name the only coach and his team to have ever beaten Lombardi in a playoff game, when, and what was the score?

10. What football power had its team honored by having the first Heisman Trophy winner to be from their team? Name that player.

11. Here are some famous numerals of college football players, mostly backs. See if you can name them. (A) #77; (B) #37; (C) #'s 41 & 35; (D) #32; (E) #44; (F) #5; (G) #98. There may be more than one famous player that wore those numbers.

12. The Cardinals of the National Football League have been in the league almost as long as the Chicago Bears—first as the Chicago Cardinals and later as the St. Louis Cardinals. They have won only one NFL title. Can you name the year they did, the team they beat, the score? Also, that backfield was known as the "million dollar" backfield. Can you name the four members of that backfield?

13. Considered to be one of the great college games of all time, the 1963 Rose Bowl game saw Southern Cal beat Wisconsin. The Badgers, trailing badly in the last quarter, fought back and almost won. Can you name the final score and the great Wisconsin passing combination that almost won the game for them? Also, name the USC passing duo that was also outstanding.

14. Since 1930, the Sullivan Award has been given to an athlete judged to be the best *amateur* athlete of the year. The first winner was Bobby Jones for golf. Only two football players have ever won the Sullivan Award. Who are they and when did they win?

15. This great player holds many records in the NFL and every time they list an All-Time All-Pro team, he is the easiest selection. He holds the record for having led the league the most times in scoring and most touchdown passes caught in a lifetime and most touchdown passes in a season. He shares that with others. Name him and the team he played for.

16. Name the teams that actually opened the first season in the American Football League. Give the city or area they represented and the nickname they played with. Also, give the year the AFL began operation—meaning playing football games.

17. Name the Heisman Trophy winners that are members of the Pro Football Hall of Fame.

18. One of the greatest college games of all time was the 1974 Sugar Bowl game between Notre Dame and Alabama. The play that kept Notre Dame alive came late in the fourth quarter. Describe what happened giving the down, the score, the play and the players that made the play work.

19. This great college halfback made All American and played in the Rose Bowl. He also was named Most Valuable Player in the American League and three times led the league in RBIs. Who is he?

20. Since they began keeping records in 1937, the NCAA has only had one person win back-to-back scoring titles. Who is he?

Answers

1. Grantland Rice, reporting for his New York newspaper's Sunday edition wrote of the Four Horsemen after watching Notre Dame beat Army in New York at the Polo Grounds, October 18, 1924. The lead in his column read as follows: "Outlined against the blue-grey October sky, the Four Horsemen rode again. In dramatic lore they were known as famine, pestilence, destruction and death. These are only aliases. Their real names are Stuldreher, Miller, Crowley and Layden." Later, the press felt that the Notre Dame line should get some credit so they were called the "Seven Mules." The captain of that great Irish team was Adam Walsh, the center and an All American.

2. Baugh, Sammy—quarterback, Washington Redskins

Bell, Bert—Founder Philadelphia Eagles, NFL Commissioner, 1946-59

Carr, Joe—President of NFL, 1921-39

Clark, Earl (Dutch)—quarterback, coach, Detroit Lions, Cleve. Rams

Grange, Harold (Red)—Halfback, Chicago Bears

Halas, George—Founder & President, Chicago Bears, player & Head Coach

Hein, Mel—center, New York Giants, 1931-45

Henry, Wilbur (Pete)—tackle, coach, Canton Bulldogs, N.Y Giants, 1921-28

Hubbard, Robert (Cal)—tackle, Giants, Packers, Pitt. Pirates, 1927-36

Hutson, Don—end, Green Bay Packers, 1935-45

Lambeau, Earl (Curly)—founder and coach, Green Bay Packers, 1921-29

Mara, Tim—founder, New York Giants

Marshall, George Preston—Founder & President of Washington Redskins

McNally, John (Johnny Blood)—halfback, 15 season with Packers, Steelers

Nagurski, Bronko—fullback, Chicago Bears

Nevers, Ernie—fullback, coach, Duluth Eskimos, Chicago Cardinal, 1926-39

Thorpe, Jim—halfback, Canton Bulldogs, first President of NFL

3. The first winner of the Jim Thorpe Trophy as the Most Valuable Player in the National Football League went to Harlon Hill, a great receiver with the Chicago Bears. The year was 1955. The player that has been awarded the Thorpe Trophy the most times is Jim Brown, the all-time leading rusher from the Cleveland Browns. He won in 1958, in 1963 (shared it with Y. A. Tittle), and in 1965.

4. In 1902, Michigan beat Stanford, 49-0.

5. In 1946, George Connor, tackle, from Notre Dame.

6. In 1937, the nation's leading passer was Davey O'Brien of Texas Christian University; the leading rusher and scorer was Bryon "Whizzer" White of Colorado. White is now the Honorable Justice Byron White of the U.S. Supreme Court.

7. The great passing combination at Alabama in 1934 was Dixie Howell to the fabled Don Hutson. The other end on that team was Paul "Bear" Bryant and Alabama beat Stanford, 29-13.

8. For CBS, Ray Scott and Jack Wittaker did the play-by-play and for NBC, Curt Gowdy and the late Paul Christman.

9. Buck Shaw coached the Philadelphia Eagles to the NFL title, in 1960, beating Lombardi's Green Bay Packers, 17-13, at Franklin Field, in Philadelphia.

10. The University of Chicago was the first school to have one of its players selected as the winner of the Heisman Trophy. The player was Jay Berwanger and the year was 1935. Chicago dropped big time football a few years later.

11. (A) #77 is the most famous. It was worn by Red Grange, the "Galloping Ghost" of Illinois. (B) #37 is the marvelous Doak Walker of Southern Methodist University and the Detroit Lions. (C) #41 & 35 belong to the fabled backfield of Glenn Davis (Mr. Outside) and Felix "Doc" Blanchard (Mr. Inside) of the great Army teams in the 1940s. (D) #32 belongs to many great players but the two most famous from their college days are Johnny Lujack of Notre Dame and O. J. Simpson of Southern California, both were Heisman Trophy winners. (E) #44 belongs to Kyle Rote of SMU, maybe the best all around athlete to come out of the Southwest Conference, #44 also belongs almost exclusively to the great backs at Syracuse University, Jim Brown, Ernie Davis, and Floyd Little. (F) #5 belongs to the "Golden Boy" of Notre Dame and the Green Bay Packers, Paul Hornung. (G) #98 is the numeral that Tom Harmon of Michigan wore, one of the greatest backs to ever play football.

12. The Chicago Cardinals beat the Philadelphia Eagles for the NFL title in 1947 by the score of 28-21. The "million dollar" backfield had Paul Christman at quarterback, Charlie Trippi and Elmer Angsman at halfbacks, and Pat Harder at fullback. The term "million dollar" backfield came when Cardinal owner, Charlie Bidwell, said he would not give up that backfield for a million dollars. In 1947, a million dollars was a lot of money.

13. Southern California won, 42-37. The Wisconsin passing combination was Ron VanderKelen

to Pat Richter. The USC combination was Pete Beathard to Hal Bedsoe.

14. In 1945, Felix "Doc" Blanchard won the Sullivan Award as the best amateur athlete in America. The next year, his teammate, Arnold Tucker, quarterback of the Army football team, was named winner. They are the only two football players to have won the Sullivan Award.

15. Don Hutson of the Green Bay Packers. He is always named at end on both the All-Time college team and the All-Time pro team.

16. Boston Patriots, Buffalo Bills, Dallas Texans, Denver Broncos, Houston Oilers, Los Angeles Chargers, New York Titans, and the Oakland Raiders. The American Football League began play in the fall of 1960.

17. There are none, as of this writing.

18. Trailing 23-17, Notre Dame had a fourth down deep in its own territory. A punt would turn the ball over to Alabama. So Notre Dame decided to go for it. They only had a few yards to make. But they gambled that Alabama would not look for a pass. Quarterback Tom Clemmens faked a run, dropped back, and hit Rich Casper near the Notre Dame 30-yard line for a first down. The Irish took it the rest of the way to win, 24-23.

19. Jackie Jensen. He was an All American halfback at California and played in the 1949 Rose Bowl. He joined the New York Yankees and was later traded to the Boston Red Sox where he was named MVP of the American League in 1958.

20. Tom Harmon of Michigan. He won the NCAA scoring title in 1939-1940.

Bart Starr of the Green Bay Packers passing in Super Bowl I. Twice MVP in the Super Bowl, Starr was inducted into the Hall of Fame the first year he was eligible. Can you name the first player who played in a Super Bowl Game to be inducted into the Hall of Fame?

Chapter 6
Super Bowl

Lamar Hunt of the Kansas City Chiefs named it, and the Commissioner of the National Football League tried to get the press to call the game the World's Professional Football championship. But Hunt's name stuck. He called it "The Super Bowl." That was back in 1966 when the men that run pro football, the owners, decided that it was time to stop the war between the old guard National Football League and the upstart American Football League. Afterall, they reasoned, paying those huge bonuses to football players was stupid when they could keep the money if they stopped fighting and banded together. And the television pie would be even bigger.

The first Super Bowl was played in Los Angeles, and it pitted the fabled Green Bay Packers of Vince Lombardi against Hunt's own team, the Kansas City Chiefs. Hunt had told the assembled press conference, when the merger was announced, that the first game between the champions of the respective leagues would be the "purest" of the games because the next year there would be a common draft, and the "bloodlines" of the leagues would be spoiled by such a draft.

Now they have played 13 of these Super Bowl games, and the intensity of the rivalry between the NFL and the AFL has been muted. The first four between the leagues found the score even—two wins for the NFL and two for the AFL. In Super Bowl V, the contestants represented the NFC and the AFC. The winner was given the Lombardi Trophy, named in honor of football's greatest coach who had died in September, 1970.

The Super Bowl has become the single biggest sports attraction in America. The television audience is in excess of one hundred million viewers, and the network that is televising the game spends more on promoting this game than all its other programming combined. By the time the players line up for the kick-off, the word 'super' has bent our ears more times than there are viewers of the game.

Most of the games have been less than memorable. Usually the defenses are so good that the offenses suffer; and the high excitement that the media builds up is almost never matched in the actual play. The first game, between Green Bay and Kansas City had great excitement and anticipation because it would finally settle the argument as to who was better—the NFL or the AFL. And they would do it on the football field, where it always is the only way to find out who is best.

The first AFL victory, the New York Jets upsetting the Baltimore Colts, brought parity to pro football. It was the biggest upset in pro football history, and Joe Namath's guarantee of a Jet victory created much greater interest in that game than was there before Namath prophesied. Everyone expected the Colts to continue the domination that Lombardi's Packers had established in the first two games.

The Jets upset in Super Bowl III was followed by the Kansas City Chiefs upset of the heavily favored Minnesota Vikings. This was the last game in the series where the teams represented the NFL and the AFL. And it was fitting that the last team to represent the AFL was the Chiefs. They represented them in the first game against the Packers and were blown out by one of the greatest teams in the history of pro football. Their victory over a favored Viking team was a fitting end to the Super Bowl as played between the NFL/AFL.

Since 1971, the NFC has been represented almost exclusively by the Dallas Cowboys and the Minnesota Vikings. The Cowboys have appeared in five of the games; the Vikings in four. In the AFC, an expansion team, the Miami Dolphins, and the Pittsburgh Steelers have dominated. The Steelers came the NFL into the AFC, along with the Cleveland Browns and Baltimore Colts to balance the two conferences. Since the days when the Packers dominated football and the Super Bowl, the Steelers, the Cowboys, and the Oakland Raiders have dominated the sport. The Dolphins were superb for a run of three seasons, but these three teams seem to have inherited the Packers' mantle. But the 1978 season showed that there are some newcomers on the scene; and maybe one day, the Rams, Oilers and others will be the target of the questions about the Super Bowl.

When Vince Lombardi was asked by a reporter how important that first Super Bowl game against the Chiefs was, the great coach answered, "I can't consider this game to be the most important my team has ever played in because we've been in so many championship games. And, there is no tradition for the game. You have to have tradition before an event can be important." The Super Bowl now has tradition, after thirteen games, and the questions that follow should be easily handled by any astute sports fan.

(1) This player is the only player that played on a losing team and was named Most Valuable Player in the Super Bowl game. Who is he, for whom did he play, and in what Super Bowl? And what was the final score?

(2) Of the thirteen Super Bowls played, only one player has been named the Most Valuable Player twice. Who is he, for whom did he play, and what Super Bowls did he play in?

(3) What player has played on the most winning teams in Super Bowl history? Name the teams he played on and who they beat.

(4) Name the player that has scored the most points in a single Super Bowl game. How many did he score and in what game?

(5) Name the player that holds the record for the highest completion percentage in a single game, over ten passes attempted?

(6) What team has scored the most points in one Super Bowl game? Give the total, which Super Bowl game, and who was the loser and the final score.

(7) This Super Bowl game has been called the "Blooper Bowl" by aficionados. The two teams set the record for most interceptions in one game and one team set the record for most fumbles. Which game was the "Blooper Bowl", what two teams played, how many interceptions were there, how

many fumbles did the record setting team commit and who was that team?

(8) When the Dallas Cowboys and Pittsburgh Steelers met in Super Bowl XIII, only one team had beaten both of them in the regular season of 1978. Who was it?

(9) Which two teams playing in a Super Bowl scored the most points? Which two scored the fewest? Give games and scores.

(10) Name the Most Valuable Player in each Super Bowl.

(11) This player was the goat of one Super Bowl loss and the hero of another Super Bowl win. Can you name him? In which game was he the goat, and in which game was he the hero?

(12) Name the sights of each of the 13 Super Bowls?

(13) This player turned around a Super Bowl game with an interception. He also holds the record for most punt returns in a game. Who is he?

(14) How many touchdowns have been scored in the 13 Super Bowls by a kickoff return? Who made it (them) and name the game(s).

(15) This back holds the Super Bowl record for the longest run from scrimmage. Who is he, how many yards did he run and against whom?

(16) Which team holds the record for most field goals attempted in a Super Bowl game? Also, which team holds the record for most field goals made in a Super Bowl game?

(17) Name the players that have played in the Super Bowls that are now in the pro football Hall of Fame.

(18) This player is now a movie star of some reknown. But in a Super Bowl, he grabbed a lot of headlines by threatening to crack the helmets of the

opposition by his special 'blow' to the head. Who is he and what actually happened to this 'terrifying' player in the game? And what was the comment of the threatened team's coach?

(19) This gifted receiver holds the record for having caught the most passes in a single Super Bowl game. Who is he, how many did he catch, and in which Super Bowl game?

(20) This player played in two Super Bowl games. He holds the record for most interceptions by an individual in the history of the Super Bowl. Who is he, how many interceptions did he effect, and in what games?

(21) Of all the quarterbacks that have started in the Super Bowls, only two had numerals below 10 on their jerseys. Who are they, for whom did they play, and in which games?

(22) How many passes that have been intercepted in a Super Bowl game have been returned for a touchdown? Who are the players that made the interceptions and in which games?

(23) Name the winning and losing coaches for each of the 13 Super Bowls.

(24) In only one Super Bowl game has a blocked punt been recovered for a touchdown. Name the game, who blocked the punt, and who recovered for what team.

(25) What player holds the Super Bowl career record for most pass receptions? How many did he catch and in how many games did he play?

Answers

(1) Chuck Howley, linebacker of the Dallas Cowboys, was named MVP in Super Bowl V. Baltimore Colts beat the Dallas Cowboys, 16-14.

(2) Bart Starr of the Green Bay Packers was named MVP in Super Bowls I and II.

(3) Marv Fleming. He played on the Green Bay Packers when they beat the Kansas City Chiefs and the Oakland Raiders; and Fleming was a member of the Miami Dolphins when they beat the Minnesota Vikings and the Washington Redskins.

(4) Don Chandler of the Green Bay Packers. He kicked four field goals and 3 extra points in the Packers' victory over the Oakland Raiders, 34-14, in Super Bowl II.

(5) Bob Griese of the Miami Dolphins. In Super Bowl VII, Griese completed 8 of 11 passes for a completion percentage of 72.7 The Dolphins beat the Washington Redskins, 14-7.

(6) The Green Bay Packers scored 35 points in Super Bowl I, beating the Chiefs, 35-10. In Super Bowl XIII, Pittsburgh had 35 to the Cowboys' 31.

(7) Super Bowl V was played between the Baltimore Colts and the Dallas Cowboys. Between them they had six interceptions, three for each team. The Baltimore Colts fumbled the ball five times.

(8) The Los Angeles Rams defeated both the Steelers and the Cowboys during the regular 1978 NFL season. The Rams lost to the Cowboys in the playoffs.

(9) The Pittsburgh Steelers and the Dallas Cowboys, playing in Super Bowl XIII, scored 66 points; 35 by the Steelers and 31 by the Cowboys. In Super Bowl VII, the Dolphins scored 14 points, beating the Redskins by 7, for a total of 21 points— the fewest in the 13 Super Bowls.

(10) From the answers to questions (1) and (2), we know that Bart Starr won the MVP for Super Bowls I & II, and Chuck Howley for Super Bowl V. So far, Bart Starr is the only double winner of the Super Bowl MVP award. Joe Namath of the New York Jets won for Super Bowl III, and Len Dawson for Super Bowl IV. Roger Staubach was named MVP in Super Bowl VI, Jake Scott of the Miami Dolphins in Super Bowl VII; Larry Czonka of the Dolphins won it the next year in Super Bowl VIII; and another big running back, Franco Harris, of the Pittsburgh Steelers won the MVP in Super Bowl IX. Harris' teammate, Lynn Swann won the MVP in Super Bowl X; and another great receiver, Fred Biletnikoff, of the Oakland Raiders won it in Super Bowl XI. Two defensive heroes of the Dallas Cowboys, Randy White and Harvey Martin, shared the MVP in Super Bowl XII. The thirteenth game in the Super Bowl series saw Terry Bradshaw of the Pittsburgh Steelers win for his record breaking performance.

(11) Earl Morrall was the quarterback of the Baltimore Colts when they lost to the New York Jets in pro football's top upset. Morrall led the Colts into Jets' territory just before the end of the first half with the Jets having only a touchdown lead. The Colts tried a "flea-flicker", and Morrall had Jimmy Orr wide open near the Jets' end zone. But even though Orr was the primary receiver, Morrall somehow did not see him and threw an interception. At the start of the second half, the Colts fumbled; the Jets recovered and kicked a field goal, pretty much putting the game out of reach. But in Super Bowl V, Morrall came off the bench to replace Johnny Unitas and bring the Colts from behind to beat the Dallas Cowboys on Jim O'Brien's field goal.

(12) Los Angeles Coliseum—Super Bowl I
Miami's Orange Bowl—Super Bowl II
Miami's Orange Bowl—Super Bowl III
Tulane Stadium, New Orleans, LA—Super Bowl IV
Miami's Orange Bowl—Super Bowl V
Tulane Stadium, New Orleans, LA—Super Bowl VI
Los Angeles Coliseum—Super Bowl VII
Rice Stadium—Super Bowl VIII
Tulane Stadium, New Orleans LA—Super Bowl IX
Miami's Orange Bowl—Super Bowl X
Rose Bowl, Pasadena, CA—Super Bowl XI
The Superdome, New Orleans, LA—Super Bowl XII
Miami's Orange Bowl—Super Bowl XIII

(13) Willie Wood of the Green Bay Packers. In Super Bowl I, the Packers only led the Kansas City Chiefs by 4 points as the second half started. After a few plays, Kansas City's Len Dawson, back to pass, had to scramble from the Packers' pass rush. He put it up, and Wood picked it off, ran to the Chiefs' 5-yard line. The Packers scored on the very next play, and it was all over. Wood returned 5 punts in Super Bowl II against the Oakland Raiders to hold that record.

(14) None. Thus far, not one kickoff has been returned for a touchdown.

(15) Tom Matte of the Baltimore Colts who ran 58 yards on one play against the New York Jets in Super Bowl III.

(16) The New York Jets attempted five field goals in Super Bowl III for the record. The Green Bay Packers made four out of four, kicked by Don Chandler, in Super Bowl II.

(17) In Super Bowl I and II, the Green Bay Packers had the following players that are now in the Hall of fame: Jim Taylor, Bart Starr, Forrest Gregg and Ray Nitchke. The Packers' great coach Vince Lombardi was inducted upon his untimely death. Weeb Ewbank, coach of the New York Jets in Super Bowl III, is a member as is Lance Alworth who played for the Dallas Cowboys in Super Bowl VI. John Unitas of the Baltimore Colts played in Super Bowls III & V.

(18) The player was Fred Williamson, now a movie actor; but in 1967 he was a cornerback with the AFL's championship team, the Kansas City Chiefs. In preparation before Super Bowl I, Williamson told the press that he had this terrible weapon that would smash the helmets of the Green Bay receivers and backs when he hit them. If the Packers were scared they didn't show it. In the fourth quarter, they ran a sweep towards Williamson's position. When the whistle blew, the Chiefs had to send the stretcher out for "the Hammer" (Williamson's nickname). Asked in the locker room after the game why it had taken the Packers so long to put Williamson out of the game, Vince Lombardi replied, "That was the first time he ever came close to trying to make a tackle."

(19) George Sauer. He caught eight passes in Super Bowl III against the Baltimore Colts in pro football's greatest upset.

(20) Chuck Howley of the Dallas Cowboys had three interceptions in two games, Super Bowls V and VI.

(21) Daryle Lamonica of the Oakland Raiders in Super Bowl II wore the number 3 on his uniform. Craig Morton of the Denver Broncos wore number 7 on his uniform in Super Bowl XII.

(22) Two. Willie Brown of the Oakland Raiders picked off a Fran Tarkenton pass in Super Bowl XI and ran it back 75 yards for a touchdown. Herb Adderley of the Green Bay Packers picked off a Daryle Lamonica pass and ran it back 60 yards for the touchdown in Super Bowl II against the Oakland Raiders.

(23)

		Winning Coach	**Losing Coach**
Super Bowl	I	Vince Lombardi	Hank Stram
Super Bowl	II	Vince Lombardi	John Rauch
Super Bowl	III	Weeb Ewbank	Don Shula
Super Bowl	IV	Hank Stram	Bud Grant
Super Bowl	V	Don McCafferty	Tom Landry
Super Bowl	VI	Tom Landry	Don Shula
Super Bowl	VII	Don Shula	George Allen
Super Bowl	VIII	Don Shula	Bud Grant
Super Bowl	IX	Chuck Noll	Bud Grant
Super Bowl	X	Chuck Noll	Tom Landry
Super Bowl	XI	John Madden	Bud Grant
Super Bowl	XII	Tom Landry	Red Miller
Super Bowl	XIII	Chuck Noll	Tom Landry

(24) In Super Bowl IX, Matt Blair of the Minnesota Vikings blocked Pittsburgh Steelers' Bobby Walton's punt. Terry Brown of the Vikings recovered it in the end zone for the Vikings only score.

(25) Chuck Foreman of the Minnesota Vikings has caught 20 passes in four appearances in the Super Bowl games.

Hamburger haven

Chapter 7
Picture Quiz

Remember those old trading cards that had pictures of our favorite ballplayers on them? You would go down to the local penny-candy store and buy a pack of bubble gum, hoping the cards in there would be of players you wanted or that you could trade for one that someone else had. If you were a Chicago Cubs fan, a Stan Hack card was worth five of Luke Appling; but if you came from the south side of Chicago, the Appling card was worth ten of any Cub.

The pictures of the players showed some kind of action stance, hitting or fielding. More often, however, the picture was a simple head and shoulder shot of our hero. Shoeboxes usually held our cards, and the really well-organized trader had the cards all organized by team and position.

One of the ways to build up your collection, besides buying bubble gum, was to lag cards against the schoolyard wall. One never lagged his favorites, but only those he was willing to lose. Very competitive games resulted with bystanders often asked to rule if one shooter's "leaner" was higher than his opponents. Some players would get some paraffin from their mom and melt it onto their cards for better sliding on the concrete or floor.

Today, trading cards is a very big business. Companies still sell bubble gum, but the players are now from all sports. Baseball is still the biggest, but football and basketball and even tennis, golf, and hockey have their great players as part of the trading card boom. Now an O.J. Simpson may be worth more than a Reggie Jackson; and Bill Walton may be worth more than a Tom Seaver. But all of us have our favorites, whether it is from the stars of today or yesterday.

The men pictured in this photo quiz are from baseball and football. All are members of their respective Hall of Fame. Each was a super star, obviously, since he is a member of the Hall of Fame. Because both Halls require a five-year waiting period before induction after the player has completed his career, some of the stars of today will not be part of the picture quiz.

But all of the men photographed here should be recognizable by their picture. To help you identify the person in each picture, a small hint is given below each one. But that hint will probably not be needed by such experts as yourself.

(1) double talk

(2) Irish railroad laborer

(3) McGraw's jewel

(4) Paul Hornung of the '30s

(5) Homo sapiens

(6) Browns' blaster

(7) Ronald Reagan played him

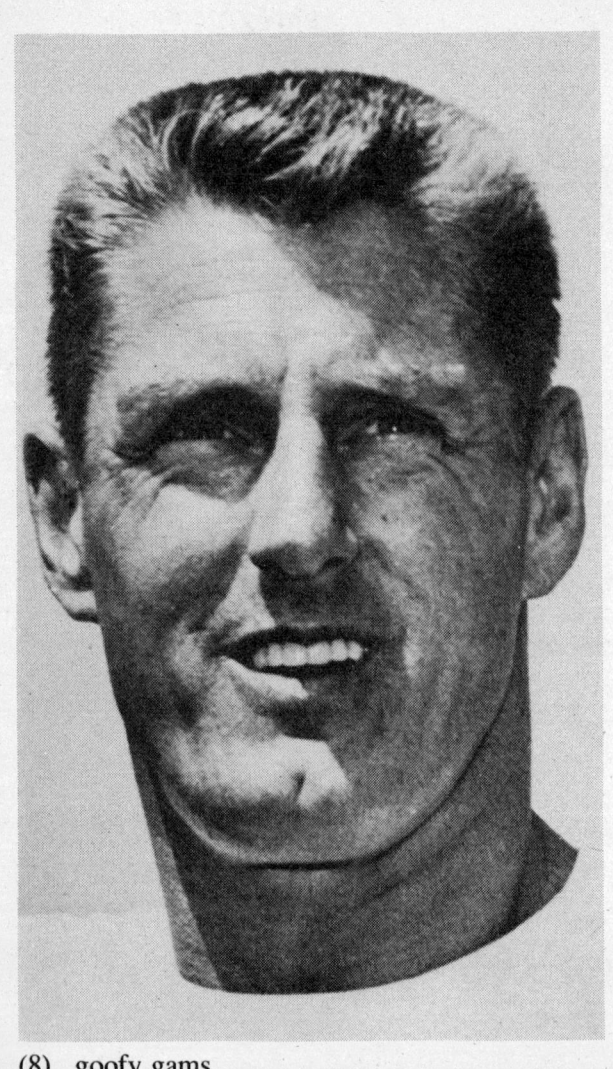

(8) goofy gams

(9) tart

(10)   win one but lose the war

(11) talk, talk, talk

(12) Pilgrim's bird

(13) port side

(14) Huck Finn's pal afraid

(15) #4

(16) rhymes with line

(17) Gang leader

(18) to Hudson before Isbell

(19) spot marked twice

(20) throw a calf by its horns

(21) light, Henry and Edsel

(22) Ol' Mother's cupboard

(23) old drinking buddies

(24) Longhorns and Lions

1. Pete Rose had all of sports excited when he set the modern day National League record for hitting in 44 consecutive games in 1978. The major league record was set by Joe DiMaggio. Can you name the number of games DiMaggio hit consecutively in, what year this happened, and the team and pitchers that finally stopped Joe. (Answer on page 191)

2. Nancy Lopez set a Ladies PGA record for winning five consecutive tournaments in 1978. Can you name the man who holds the PGA record, what year he set it, and how many PGA tournaments he won in a row? (Answer on page 191)

3. Steve Cauthen won the Triple Crown in 1978 riding Affirmed. Is he the youngest jockey to have ever won the Triple Crown? If not, who is? (Answer on page 191)

4. Bjorn Borg won his fourth consecutive Wimbledon title in 1979. Only one player since World War I has won three Wimbledon titles in a row, besides Borg. Can you name him? And the years he did it? (Answer on page 191)

(25) no hint needed

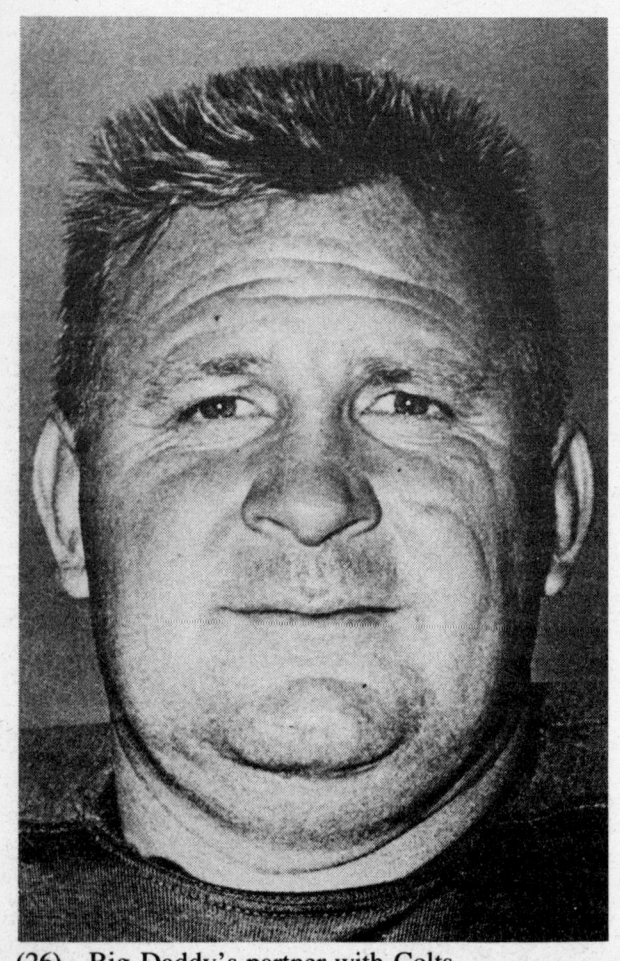

(26) Big Daddy's partner with Colts

(27) started "Williams' shift"

(28) "Dutch"

(29) #9

(30) Duke's greatest & Halas'

Answers

(1) Casey Stengel was a great ball player himself, but he became better known as the only manager to ever win five consecutive World Series, done with the New York Yankees from 1949-1954. His conversations with the press in those years led to the term "Stengeleese," because he'd double-talk the writers in his own special Casey Stengel way.

(2) Paddy Driscoll was a great running back with the Chicago Cardinals in the 1920s. He later worked with the rival Chicago Bears and even coached them when George Halas made one of his retirements. The nickname Paddy comes from the term given to Irish immigrants that worked on the railroads during our nation's move west.

(3) Mel Ott came to John McGraw's New York Giants as a youngster just 18 years old. McGraw saw greatness in this left-handed hitter that lifted his right leg as the pitch came in and ended up hitting over 500 home runs in his career.

(4) Johnny Blood is actually John McNally, but he took the name Blood from a theatre marquee advertising Douglas Fairbanks Sr. in the silent movie, "Blood and Sand." Blood was a great running back and also a fabulous party-goer in his heyday.

(5) Stan Musial is Homo sapiens or "The Man," as he was known to baseball fans. Tradition says that Musial was given that nickname by Brooklyn Dodger fans after he had had one of his typical Musial hitting days in Ebbets Field.

(6) Marion Motley was Paul Brown's great fullback in Cleveland. When the defenses would put great pressure on passer Otto Graham, Brown would call a draw play for Motley and the great fullback would blast up the middle for a long gain.

(7) Christy Mathewson was one of baseball's greatest pitchers and a fine athlete in other sports. Ronald Reagan played him in the movie story of Mathewson's life.

(8) Elroy Hirsh was one of the premier runners in college football and in the pros, he converted to wide receiver with the Rams. His nickname was "Crazy Legs."

(9) Bob Lemon was a Hall of Famer from the Cleveland Indians. He was a great pitcher who managed the Yankees to a World Series title in 1978.

(10) Cliff Battles was a sensational running back and also an excellent passer with the Washington Redskins in the 1930s.

(11) Gabby Hartnett got his nickname because he was always talking to the batters. He was the greatest catcher in Chicago Cubs' history.

(12) Turk Edwards starred as a tackle with the Washington Redskins, going both ways. He was a huge man for those days, weighing over 250 lbs.

(13) Lefty Gomez was nicknamed "Goofy" after the Walt Disney character because he was a southpaw and also a real character.

(14) Tom Fears teamed with his Hall of Fame buddy, Elroy Hirsh, to form one of football's greatest receiving combinations.

(15) Lou Gehrig had one of the most famous numerals in sports, number 4. His number has been retired by the Yankees.

(16) Mel Hein came out of Washington State and played all-pro center for the New York Giants for a decade and a half in the 1930s and mid '40s.

(17) Frank Frisch was the manager and second baseman on one of baseball's legendary teams, the Gashouse Gang of the St. Louis Cardinals. Frisch was nicknamed the Fordham Flash

(18) Arnie Herber was the Green Bay Packers star tailback in the 1930s passing to the great Don Hudson. He was also a fine runner.

(19) Jimmy Foxx, nicknamed "Double X", once hit 58 home runs in a single season.

(20) "Bulldog" Turner of the Chicago Bears became the prototype of the modern day center in the 'T' formation; big, strong and quick.

(21) Whitey Ford holds many World Series pitching records.

(22) Cal Hubbard is the only man to be in both Halls of Fame.

(23) Joe Cronin was a great hitter and fine fielder at shortstop.

(24) Bobby Layne came out of Texas as an All American for the Longhorns and then led the Detroit Lions to two NFL back-to-back titles in 1952 and 1953.

(25) Ty Cobb is considered by most experts to be the greatest all-around player in baseball history.

(26) Art Donovan was defensive tackle on one of pro football's greatest defensive teams, the Baltimore Colts, in the late '50s.

(27) Lou Boudreau was a great hitter and fielder with the Cleveland Indians but as their manager, he came up with the "Williams shift" to stop the great Ted Williams.

(28) Earl "Dutch" Clark, super star in the early thirties with the Detroit Lions.

(29) Ted Williams wore number 9 for the Boston Red Sox.

(30) George McAfee came out of Duke to become the premier breakaway runner in pro football for George Halas and the Chicago Bears in the 1940s.

This Robert Riger drawing of the marvelous Bob Cousy captures the dedication and intensity of one of basketball's all-time greats. What college did Cousy play for and what team first drafted him in the pros?

Chapter 8
Basketball

When Dr. James Naismith was told by his superior at the International Young Men's Christian Association Training School in Springfield, Massachusetts to find a sport that the students could play during the winter, little did Naismith know his invention would become the American game. Baseball and football have their genesis in sports from other parts of the world. But basketball is strictly American. And today, it has become one of the most popular sports around the world.

The first known game was in December of 1891 at the Springfield YMCA. Naismith had originally designed his new game with boxes to catch the ball, but he could not find the right size so he got a couple of baskets made of wood and nailed them at opposite ends of the gym to the balcony parapet. Naismith's original rules did not provide for the dribble, but players quickly figured out how to keep the ball within one of his rules. That rule forbid running with the ball but allowed passing from one player to another. Nothing was said about a player passing to himself so some long-forgotten, enterprising player bounced the ball and kept bouncing as he ran up the court, actually passing the ball to himself. Naismith quickly saw the beauty of the new maneuver and incorporated it into the rules. One wonders if those early players could handle the ball like a Bob Cousy or Doctor J?

Over the years basketball has become the game of the people. You don't need a lot of equipment and a big field to play; and one person can enjoy himself, just shooting baskets—whether the basket is hung in a huge fieldhouse or on some macadam court or even over the old garage door. It is the city game and the farm game—as popular on the streets of New York or Los Angeles as it is in the farms and hamlets of Indiana and Kentucky or North Carolina.

Basketball is the game of the schools and clubs. Great fame can come to a school or college with a winning team, and the school doesn't have to foot the bill for the scholarships necessary for football. Five good players and you can be national champs, state champs or whatever. Some of the best players of all time played at small schools.

College basketball began in the east as did pro basketball, but soon the sport spread across the country. The first intercollegiate game was actually played in Minnesota, however, most historians credit Yale with being the school that spread basketball among the colleges.

The first recorded pro game took place in Trenton, New Jersey, and the players split the take with each one getting $15 after expenses. The captain got $16. The most famous pro team at the turn of the century was the Buffalo Germans, and their player/coach was Forrest C. "Phog" Allen. They won over 800 games in their 30-year existence. After World War I, the Original Celtics became the power of pro basketball and played across the country. They were a New York team and some of the greatest players of the early days of pro basketball were on their team. Players like Nat Holman, "Dutch" Dehnert, Joe Lapchick and Johnny Beckman made the Original Celtics the talk of basketball. And until the Minneapolis Lakers came along after World War II, the Original Celtics were the best draw in pro basketball, next to the Harlem Globetrotters. And nothing has ever been the draw the Trotters were and are today.

The college game really didn't have the national interest that college football had in the '20s and '30s But an enterprising young sportswriter got Madison Square Garden to agree to put six of the best college teams in the east into a triple-header. The sportswriter was Ned Irish, and the promotion filled the Garden. That was in 1931. In 1934 Irish went into basketball promotion full time, and college basketball became as big an item at Madison Square Garden as hockey and boxing. In 1938 Irish promoted the first major college basketball tournament in the country, the National Invitational Tournament. The NCAA, seeing the success of the NIT, started their own tournament in 1939 to select the collegiate champion of the year.

Dr. Naismith died in 1939, but he saw his game grow in popularity and the players skill at playing his game go far beyond anything he had envisioned when he followed his superior's instruction. But one must wonder what he would think of today's game with "slam-dunks," jump shots, zone-presses, four-corner offense and all the marvelous things that have happened to the game over the years. And we can only imagine how the good Doctor would thrill watching any of the great UCLA teams, the Celtics of Cousy and Russell, the artistry of Erving, West, Jabbar, Pettit, Mikan, Robertson or Havlicek and all the wonderful players that have entertained basketball fans over the years.

Basketball has a great tradition and many wonderful athletes have played the game, and some outstanding individuals have coached the sport. The following questions will deal with the memorable moments in basketball history and the records and people that make basketball the sport of America.

1. The American Basketball Association completed its first season in what year; which team was their champion, and which team was the runner-up?

2. The National Basketball Association established its Most Valuable Player award in 1956. Name the player that won the first MVP award, and the name of the player who has won it the most times, and how many times?

3. Name the first team George Mikan played with in pro basketball.

4. This man is the only man in the Basketball Hall of Fame to be named twice—once as a player and then again as a coach. Give the school he played at which first gave him his election and the school he coached at for which he was rehonored.

5. Name the only team to win the NIT title and the NCAA title in the same season. Who coached that team?

6. From 1964 until 1974, UCLA won every NCAA title except one. Name the team that won that year, name the year, and the team that was the runner-up.

7. The Helms College Player of the Year began in 1924. The Helms Foundation has an award that it gives each year to the basketball player they think is the best player of that season. Name the player(s) awarded the Helms award three times, and name the school(s) where he (they) played.

8. In the early 1960s these two basketball players dominated college basketball, and their careers involved them playing against each other and, later in the pros, as teammates. One player came from the streets of a major city; the other from the security of family wealth. *Hint:* one replaced the other as the starting forward on the pro team. Who are they, and for what college teams did they play, and on what pro team were they teammates?

9. This basketball player stunned the establishment of Eastern basketball with his running and shooting in a game in Madison Square Garden. His style of play is credited with changing the face of offensive basketball. Who is he, for whom did he play, and what team from the east did they beat?

10. The only player to score 100 points in a professional basketball game is Wilt Chamberlain. However, there were three other players that scored 30 or more points in that game and they all belonged to the opposition. Name the three players, the team they played for, and what other record did Chamberlain set in that game besides total points?

11. This team was nicknamed the "Whiz Kids." Can you name this team? Can you give (approximately) when they played?

12. What school has supplied the most players to the NBA in its history?

13. Which coach has won the most games in college basketball? Which coach in pro basketball? Which coach has won the most NCAA titles?

14. Name the teams that have gone undefeated in a single basketball season, including the NCAA title. Can you give the year for each?

15. Name the college player that scored the most points in a single game, how many, and against whom.

16. Who was the first player in pro basketball history to score over 20,000 points in his career? For whom did he play?

17. From 1958 until 1966 the Boston Celtics won eight straight National Basketball Association championships. Since then, only one team has won the NBA title back-to-back. Name that team and the years they won consecutive titles.

18. What college player holds the NCAA record for most points scored in his college career? Name the school where he played.

19. Name the player who has played the most consecutive games in NBA history and the team he played with.

20. In 1962 the Associated Press began an award for the NBA Coach of the Year. Name the coach(es) that have won the award more than once.

Answers

1. The American Basketball Association completed their first season in 1968. Pittsburgh played New Orleans in the first ABA championship series; Pittsburgh won, four games to three.

2. Bob Pettit, the genuine great forward of the St. Louis Hawks, won the NBA Most Valuable Player award in 1956, the first year it was awarded. Since then Bill Russell of the Boston Celtics has won the award five times, and Kareem Abdul-Jabbar of the Milwaukee Bucks and now of the Los Angeles Lakers has won it five times.

3. The great George Mikan first played pro basketball with the Chicago American Gears, a team in the National Basketball League; that was 1945-46. The owner of the Gears tried to start his own league built around Mikan and his teammates, but it folded; and Mikan was picked up by the Minneapolis Lakers, when they took his name out of a hat that was being used by the owners to select the players from the Gears for their teams.

4. John R. Wooden is the only twice-honored member of the Basketball Hall of Fame. He was an outstanding college player at Purdue in the early 1930s being named by the Helms Foundation All-Time All American and the Grantland Rice All Time team in 1953. From 1948, as the coach of the UCLA Bruins, he established the greatest coaching record in college history, winning ten NCAA titles. Wooden was inducted into the Basketball Hall of Fame as a player in 1959 and rehonored as a coach in 1972.

5. City College of New York (CCNY) is the only team to have ever won the NIT championship and the NCAA title in the same season; that was in

1950. The coach of the CCNY team was Nat Holman, the legendary star of the Original Celtics and member of the Basketball Hall of Fame.

6. In 1966, Texas Western won the NCAA title. They beat a heavily favored Kentucky team, 72-65. Texas Western today is known as the University of Texas, El Paso. None of those players ever made the pros.

7. Lew Alcindor, playing for UCLA, won the Helms College Player of the Year in 1967, '68 and '69. Alcindor is now known as Kareem Abdul-Jabbar. Bill Walton of UCLA also won the Helms award three times, in 1972, '73, and shared the award with David Thompson of North Carolina State in 1974.

8. Cazzie Russell came from the macadam playgrounds of Chicago and went to the University of Michigan where he led the Wolverines to basketball greatness. Because of Russell, a new fieldhouse was built on the campus so that the new Michigan basketball fans could watch their team. Russell was an All American twice and won the Helms College player of the Year in 1966. He was the number one draft choice of the New York Knicks and became their starting forward in 1967.

The other player was Bill Bradley. He came from the wealth of a banking family in the St. Louis area. Like Russell, Bradley's play sparked basketball interest at Princeton, and he led them to three Ivy League titles. Helms College Player of the Year in 1965, Bradley was drafted by the New York Knicks but passed up pro ball to become a Rhodes Scholar. After two years at Oxford, Bradley came home and signed with the Knicks. The next year he replaced Russell as the starting forward on those great Knicks teams of Reed, DeBusschere, and Frazier.

9. Angelo "Hank" Luisetti came east with the Stanford University Indians to play Long Island University in Madison Square Garden. LIU was considered to be the number one team in the country. They had a 43-game winning streak and were coached by one of the greatest coaches in basketball history, Clair Bee. Luisetti showed Bee and the rest of the more than 18,000 fans at the Garden a new style of basketball with his one-handed shot and his passing and driving. The Stanford team won 45-31, a rout in those days. LIU went on to win 26 more straight games using the Luisetti influence which changed the face of offensive basketball.

10. On the night of March 2, 1962, the Philadelphia Warriors played the New York Knicks in Hershey, Pennsylvania. Wilt Chamberlain, the greatest scorer in NBA history went on a personal fling and scored 100 points. It was and is a feat never before matched. In that game, three Knicks scored over 30 points each—Richie Guerin had 39, Buckner scored 33, and Willie Naulis had 31. Records indicate that this is the only time three players on the same team scored over thirty points each. Also, the record for most free throws made in one game is 28, and Wilt Chamberlain set that mark in this game. He made 28 out of 32 attempts. Fans remembering the suffering Chamberlain went through later in his career when he had to make a free throw will be astounded that Wilt shot .875% from the free throw line in that game.

11. The "Whiz Kids" were the starting five at the University of Illinois. They played in 1942 and 1943 and won the Big Ten Title in 1943. After the war, they reunited in 1946 and won the Big Ten again. Their leader was All American Andy Phillip.

12. UCLA

13. Adolph Rupp of Kentucky holds the record for most victories; 874 victories against only 190 losses for an astounding .821 winning percentage. Arnold J. "Red" Auerbach is the winningest coach in pro basketball (in all of basketball for that matter), having recorded over 1,000 victories in his career as a pro coach with the Washington Caps, Tri-Cities and, from 1950-1966, the Boston Celtics. John Wooden at UCLA has won the most NCAA titles—ten—a record that may never be matched.

14. 1956—San Francisco University   29-0
    1957—North Carolina University   32-0
    1964—UCLA   30-0
    1972—UCLA   30-0
    1973—UCLA   30-0
    1976—Indiana University   32-0

Long Island University went undefeated in 1939 but did not play in the NCAA playoffs. Army won 15 and lost 0 in 1945 but did not participate in the NCAA. Kentucky won 25 and lost 0 in 1954 but was ineligible to play in the NCAA.

15. Frank Selvy of Furman University scored 100 points against Newberry College in 1954. Bevo Francis of Rio Grande College scored more than 100 points in a game, but his record was not recognized by the NCAA.

16. Bob Pettit of the St. Louis Hawks was the first player in NBA history to score over 20,000 points in his career. He was named to the Basketball Hall of Fame and to the All Time NBA All Star team. He also was a great rebounder and an inspiration to his team.

17. The Boston Celtics. They won in 1967-68 and 1968-69. Their coach was player/coach Bill Russell. No team since then has repeated as back-to-back NBA champions.

18. Pete Maravich of Louisiana State University holds the NCAA record for points scored in a career—3667—an average of 44.2 for the 83 games he played at LSU.

19. John Kerr of the Syracuse Nats, Philadelphia and Baltimore, played in 844 consecutive games from Oct. 31, 1954 to Nov. 4, 1965.

20. Interestingly enough, no coach has ever won the Associated Press Coach of the Year twice.

Chapter 9
Words Rules and Signals

Most of us are familiar with the rules of sports and with the terminology used by writers, broadcasters and players to describe what happened. The tremendous exposure we have to sports today has lifted the veil of mystery from those "in-terms" that athlete as well as reporter thought would add a little awe in the public's mind about how difficult it was to play and understand a particular sport. Everyone knows what a "blitz" is, but when it was first introduced, football coaches, trying to explain it to the press, acted as if they had hold of special knowledge and only those mentally competent to understand atomic physics could understand football terms.

Broadcasters also like to sometimes drop a term or explain a seldom used rule to the listener, and you can almost see the smug look they have as they explain to us poor non-experts what the "inside" of the game is all about. Well, most sports fans are far more knowledgeable about sports and the jargon and rules than given credit for by the media. Most of us could turn off the sound of a football, basketball or baseball game, just watch the action, and know everything that happened, who did it, and how it was done. We really don't need to be told that when a receiver drops a pass, time is out and the pass is incomplete or that when a referee grabs his left wrist with his right hand and pulls down, he is signaling holding.

But there are some terms and rules that are used in the everyday parlance of sports that can be a minor problem in interpretation. So the following quiz should not pose a difficult problem for experts like yourself. Give the sports meaning of the word or phase, and the correct interpretation of the rule involved or what infraction the referee is signaling.

1. Acey Ducey—give sport and define.
2. In basketball, the referee blows his whistle, stops play, and places his hands on his hips. What foul is he signaling?
3. The pass receiver has caught the ball and is racing for the end zone. But he somehow drops the ball, and it rolls across the goal line, through the end zone and out. What is the ruling?
4. Belly Back—give sport and define.
5. In football, the referee blows his whistle to stop play and indicates a penalty. He faces the crowd, then turns his back, puts his right hand and arm behind his back, and makes an up and down motion with his hand and arm. What is he signaling?
6. There are men on first and third. The manager signals for a double steal. However, the lead runner from third is thrown out at home, but the relay to second base is late and the runner from first slides in safely. Is he credited with a stolen base?

7. Biathlon—define.

8. Chicken fight—name the sport and define the phrase.

9. In hockey, the referee blows play to a halt, skates to the penalty box, and, grabbing his right wrist with his left hand, he pulls the right arm down until the elbow touches his hip. What penalty is he signaling?

10. Cincinnati—name the sport and define the term.

11. Decathlete—define.

12. A batter hit the ball down the right field line. The right fielder chases it and catches it as he hits the fence. The ball pops out of his glove into the stands in fair territory. Is it a home run? What is the rule?

13. In football, the referee faces the stands and places his right hand palm down next to his throat. He then makes an outward motion and repeats two or three times. What is he signaling?

14. Key—give sport(s) and define.

15. The Turk—give sport and meaning.

16. Lift pass—name sport and define term.

17. Necessary line—name sport and define term.

18. Let's say that the Packers are playing the Cowboys and the Packers attempt a field goal. Because time is almost out in the game, the Packers decide to try the field goal on second down. The Cowboys block the attempt, and the Packers recover. They call time-out and there is still time on the clock. Which team gets the ball and why?

19. Morning line—sport(s) and define term.

20. The batter hits the ball very sharply down the foul line. The ball lands, and the umpire nearest the line moves both arms in a sweeping motion away from the fielder. What is he signaling?

21. Natation—define.

22. Palm ball—name the sport and define the term.

23. In hockey, the referee blows his whistle and then signals the penalty by rotating his hands in a circle in front of him. What penalty is he signaling?

24. Rabbit—name sport(s) and define term.

25. Voodoo ball—sport and definition of term.

Answers

1. Acey Ducey—Horse Racing. It means that the right stirrup is shorter than the left so that the jockey can more easily equalize his weight on the horse in the turns.

2. He is signaling a blocking foul.

3. Since the impetus was supplied by the offensive team, its fumble through the end zone is treated in the same manner as a kickoff through the end zone; the defensive team gets the ball at their own 20, and the fumble is treated as a touchback.

4. Belly back—action of a running back, who after getting the handoff from the quarterback, goes away from the line of scrimmage in a small half circle as he watches the blocking set up. Usually used on a power sweep or halfback option.

5. Illegal forward pass.

6. No. It is a double steal play, and if one of the runners is thrown out, the other cannot be credited with a stolen base.

7. Biathlon—athletic contest in which competitors ski over a 20-kilometer cross-country course stopping at a designated point or points to fire a rifle at stationary targets. The contest is a race against the clock and the competitors have added time to their total for missed targets.

8. Chicken fight—football. A term used to describe the action between linemen when pass blocking, especially when the pass play calls for a straight drop back by the quarterback.

9. Hooking.

10. Cincinnati—a bowling term used to describe a split that leaves the 8 and 10 pins standing.

11. Decathelete—Track and Field; An athlete who competes in the decathlon.

12. It is a ground rule double. The impetus of the ball into the bleachers is from the fielder, and, therefore, the batter cannot be given a home run.

13. Illegal motion.

14. Key—in basketball, the reference to the position near the basket where the center usually takes up his position. In football, it means the reference that the players, both offensive and defensive, use as they read the movement of the opposition.

15. The Turk is the name given by pro football players to the man who comes around to tell the player he has been cut from the team.

16. Lift Pass: Hockey. A term for one player making a long flip pass down the ice.

17. Necessary Line—Football. It is the line downfield that the offense must reach to make another first down or score, depending on the field position when they are given a first down. In other words, the necessary line, if the offense has made a first down on the defense's 23-yard line, would be the defense's 13-yard line.

18. If the Cowboys blocked the field goal attempt and the officials ruled that they had blocked it *behind* the line of scrimmage, then the Packers would keep control of the ball. In kicking a field goal with a down remaining and having it blocked behind the line of scrimmage, the rules treat the attempt as a running play or incomplete passing play, and the down is now third down. If the ball that was kicked went past the line of scrimmage, it would belong to the Cowboys no matter who fell on it. Reason—once a team kicks the ball, it is assumed they intend to give it up, unless they make the field goal.

19. Morning Line—horse racing. The probable odds for a given race estimated by the track handicapper and posted before the start of betting.

For major football games, like the Super Bowl, the term is sometimes used but it is used incorrectly.

20. A foul ball.

21. Natation—The art of swimming.

22. Palm Ball—baseball. The art of throwing the ball by the pitcher where the ball is held between the thumb and the palm instead of the pressure of the fingers. It is thrown so that the fingers do not give any rotation to the ball, and the effect is that the ball floats and is at the mercy of the winds. A very hard ball to control and even more difficult to hit.

23. Charging.

24. Rabbit—in golf, a player that must qualify each week to play on the professional golf weekly tournaments. In track and field, the "rabbit" is the runner that sets the pace, sometimes to allow a teammate to go for a record because of the fast pace the "rabbit" sets. In dog racing, it is often the name given to the mechanical lure that the dogs chase.

25. Voodoo Ball—Baseball. The term given to a baseball manufactured in the United States but stitched in Haiti.

I was responsible for two major changes in the rules in the sport in which I owned a franchise. Many feel that these changes saved my sport in its early days. What were those two major changes, what was the name of the team I owned, when did these changes take place and who am I?

Chapter 10
Who Am I?

Most sports fans know some interesting biographical information about our heroes. It could be where they were born or went to school, what handicap they might have overcome, or records they set while playing. And if they are famous enough, all the fan has to hear are a couple of phrases, and he can tell you about whom you're talking.

If a guy were to say that this athlete came from Alabama and wore #12, right away the name Joe Namath would be the answer. Or if someone were to mention that this athlete was born in Baltimore and played for the Yankees, the most likely answer would be Babe Ruth even though there have been others from Baltimore that played for the Yankees.

In this little quiz biography, some of the athletes are easily identifiable, while there might be some questions about others. The aim is to give some facts about our personality without making it too easy or too difficult. In some cases, the sport they played is identified, in others, to make it a little more difficult, you'll have to guess the sport from the clues given.

Most of the personalities are from football and baseball, since they are our major sports. But there are some biographies of others and, in every case, all are great athletes. Let us see how many of these 50 famous athletes you can identify.

1) I was 17 years old when I signed my first professional baseball contract. 16 days later, I pitched three innings against the great Gashouse Gang of the St. Louis Cardinals. I struck out eight Cardinals. In my first start in the majors, a month later, I struck out 15; and three weeks later, I set the American League record of 17 strikeouts in a single game. I am the only pitcher to have pitched a no-hitter on opening day. But my greatest disappointment is that I never won a World Series game. I was inducted into baseball's Hall of Fame the first time I was eligible. Who am I?

2) I played college football at a small eastern Ivy League-type school. I made All America and played pro football where I also made All Pro. I am a member of both the college and professional football Hall of Fame; and while playing professional football, I was able to complete my medical studies. Today, I practice medicine in the Los Angeles area. I was a lineman and went both ways, in college and the pros. Who am I?

3) I grew up in Chicago; and although I was not a good athlete, I loved being involved in sports. I became a promoter and in 1926 put together a team that barnstormed across the country. This team over the years has been seen by more people in the world than any other team or organization in the history of sports. In the 1930s and '40s we filled arenas across

the country and helped the growth of a sport into the major attraction that it is today. They made a motion picture about me and my team. (Dane Clark played me.) Who am I?

4) When I was playing, people considered me the greatest player in the history of my sport. I had a terrible temper and one time, after a fight with some opposition players, the Commissioner of the league suspended me from the playoffs. The fans were so mad they stormed the league office, burned the Commissioner in effigy, and brought the whole city to a standstill. I have held almost all the scoring records in my sport at one time or another, but I'm best remembered for the excitement I created wherever I played. Who am I?

5) I grew up in Green Bay, Wisconsin and was a star high school football player there. My high school coach was Curly Lambeau. He pointed me to Notre Dame where I played under Knute Rockne. After I left Notre Dame, I stayed in coaching until I entered the Navy in World War II. One of the players I coached was Vince Lombardi. I was immortalized in a story written by Grantland Rice after he had seen Notre Dame play. Who am I?

6) I came into baseball as a pitcher, but an injury to the shoulder of my pitching arm almost ended my career. My minor league manager took in my wife and me and talked me into trying to make it as an outfielder. He thought I was a pretty good hitter. When I retired from baseball, some twenty years later, I had won every batting title possible—from most hits to highest batting average. Only one title evaded me during my career. I never led the league in home runs. Who am I?

7) In 1948, at the United States Olympic trials, I was considered to be the surest winner in my spe-

cialties. I was the world's record holder and had not been defeated in a year. But I was beaten in both events. However, I made our team by taking the third place spot on the 100-meter dash team. And I won the Gold Medal that fall in the 100-meter. Who am I?

8) I failed to make my high school basketball team when I was a freshman and sophomore. By my senior year I was All State and then led the nation in scoring in college and was an All American. In the pros I was the first player in history to score over 20,000 points during his career. I am one of ten players to be selected on the All-Time NBA All Star team. I scored 19 of my team's 20 points in the 4th quarter as we beat the Boston Celtics for the NBA title. Who am I?

9) As an amateur, I had the Masters championship in my grasp when Arnold Palmer came from nowhere to beat me. No amateur has even come as close to winning that title. When I turned pro, immediate stardom was predicted for me. I did win some big tournaments but suffered a serious hand injury. In 1964, I won the U.S. Open, playing 36 holes in over 100 degree weather in what the experts have since called "the most courageous round of golf ever played." I retired as a touring pro and now cover golf as a broadcaster. Who am I?

10) I was nicknamed "the Man of Steel", and as a fighter, I held the middleweight title twice. Although most of my prime days as a fighter were spent in the Navy during World War II, when I came out, I participated in a series of title fights that experts have called "the greatest in boxing history." I retired after losing my title the second time and have been involved in youth work in Chicago. I am in the boxing Hall of Fame. Who am I?

11) I grew up in St. Louis and played baseball whenever I could. I joined the New York Yankees organization, and in 1948, they brought me up to the big club. Nobody gave me a chance to stick, but I did and went on to be named Most Valuable Player three times in my career. I have been a manager—winning pennants twice. Many people consider me one of the best clutch hitters in the history of the game, especially in the World Series. Who am I?

12) When I first came into the NBA, I was not wanted by the coach of the team that had "selected" me. But after 13 years in the league, he learned to accept me. My fellow players say that I was the player most responsible for bringing the fans into the arenas to watch us play. I have been named to the All-Time NBA All Star team. When youngsters playing in the schoolyard make a fancy play with the basketball, often the other players will kid them about trying to play like me. Who am I?

13) I weighed about 150 lbs. when I played tackle at Notre Dame. I was not a starter, but my coach was Knute Rockne and I studied how he coached. Later, I was an assistant at Fordham and one of my players was Vince Lombardi. As a head coach, I compiled one of the greatest winning records in modern football, and most experts consider my 1947 team to be the greatest in the history of college football. I have coached four Heisman trophy winners. Who am I?

14) I won over 300 games as a pitcher and was elected to the baseball Hall of Fame the first time I was eligible. One of the reasons I had the chance to win so many games was that I was an outstanding hitter for a pitcher. I pitched in three World Series and was considered to have one of the best pick-off moves in all of baseball. Who am I?

15) I failed to make the United States Olympic team the first time I entered the team trials. I paid my way to Tokyo and watched a Russian win my specialty—the decathlon. That was the first time an American had not won the decathlon since the Olympics resumed after World War II. In 1968, in Mexico City, I won the decathlon and set a new world record. Who am I?

16) I was born in Alabama but my family moved to Detroit because there was work up there. I became interested in boxing but never told my mother because she was against any kind of violence. I fought for over three decades and only lost 3 times in 71 fights. When I would fight, I'd fill every stadium or arena; and because of me, tickets for one of my fights cost $100, setting up the high price of tickets for today's title fights. Who am I?

17) I was considered the greatest all-around athlete to ever play in California high schools. In college, I was an all-America in football, baseball and track. I won the Heisman Trophy. One spring I led my school to victory in a track meet in the morning and hit the game-winning home run that afternoon for our baseball team. I am best known as one half of the most famous backfield combination in college football. I also played with the Los Angeles Rams. Who am I?

18) I was a sports star at the University of Kentucky but quit school to play pro baseball. But I became rich and famous in a sport that television has turned into a side-show; strictly entertainment with "good-guys" and "bad-guys". I developed a grip on my opponents that led to the writers giving me my nickname of "Strangler". I made over 3 million dollars and lost only 33 bouts in over 6,200 matches. Who am I?

19) I am considered by the experts to be one of the greatest tennis players of all time. I led the United States to a Davis Cup victory over Australia, and I have won at Wimbleton and the United States Open. When I turned pro, the tour did not make much money; so I played 58 matches in 75 days against the leading pros of those days, and we filled most places where we played. I beat Bobby Riggs, Pancho Gonzales, Lou Hoad, Ken Rosewall and others of that strength to be professional champion for many years. Who am I?

20) Many people consider me the greatest athlete in the history of sports. My name is Edson-Arantes do Nascimento. I have been awarded the French Legion of Honor and have had audiences with Popes and Kings and Queens. When I played, riots sometimes took place; and when I led my nation to the world's championship, the country celebrated for a week. A few years ago, I signed a contract for 4.7 million dollars to come out of retirement and play for three more years. This made me the highest-paid team athlete in the history of sports. Who am I?

21) I was the most highly recruited basketball player in the country when I finished my high school career. I stayed in my home state and led the state university to an NCAA championship and consecutive conference championships my three years of eligibility. I did not play pro ball the first year after graduation; but the next year, when I joined the NBA, I was Rookie of the Year. I have been named to a number of NBA All Pro teams during my career and was one time voted the MVP in the All-Star game. I played on one NBA championship team and have been considered one of the best outside shooters in the history of the NBA for a big man. I also wrote a book about memory. Who am I?

22) I first played major league baseball for the New York Yankees where I earned my nickname because I wasn't respectful enough to the great players they had at that time. The Yankees traded me to Cincinnati, and then I was traded to St. Louis where I joined the famed Gashouse Gang of the Cardinals. But it was as a manager that I gained my greatest fame. I managed both teams in the most famous rivalry in baseball, had fights with fans, umpires and players—on my team as well as on the opposition. I was suspended for one year—but most knowledgeable people still consider me one of the best managers of a team that is fighting for a pennant. Who am I?

23) I am the only player to have ever won the Heisman Trophy while playing on a team that had a losing season. I was the "bonus" choice in the NFL that year and played without distinction my first three years. But my career turned around; and, for the next six years, I was part of what most experts consider the greatest football team in history. I was MVP in the NFL one season and led the league in scoring a number of years. Who am I?

24) I was so awkward and clumsy as a youngster that nobody wanted me on their team no matter what sport I tried to play. I didn't have an athletic scholarship when I went to college, but my coach worked with me to teach me how to shoot and develop better coordination. By the time I retired from basketball, I was voted the greatest player in the history of the game. Because of me, the rules of the game were changed. The three-second rule was introduced, and the width of the lanes was widened to keep me away from the basket. Who am I?

25) As a rookie in my sport, I earned more than six million dollars for my employers. I learned my

trade on my folks' farm in Kentucky; and when I was 16, one of the greats in my business came to watch me and told my dad that he could find few faults with my style. I am only one of ten in my profession to have been part of the greatest achievement our business offers a competitor. And this competition has been going on each year since 1900. Who am I?

26) I am one of two players in the history of the National League to have been named the Most Valuable Player three times. I am a member of baseball's Hall of Fame, and many experts consider me to have been one of the very best at fielding my position. I possessed a strong throwing arm; and as a batter, I was both a home run and high average hitter. My personality was best described by a writer who said that "he is always happy." I replied, when questioned as to why I was always smiling: "being paid to play baseball, to do what I love, Man, that's happiness!"

27) I had a good career at the University of Kentucky and was drafted by the Chicago Bears. I played quarterback and sometimes linebacker for them. After ten years, the Bears let me go and nobody in the NFL picked me up. So I joined the American Football League where I played until I retired, involuntarily, in 1975. By that time the two leagues had merged. I have never been named Most Valuable Player, but I hold many NFL records. Who am I?

28) I recently retired from my sport after being one of its most famous players. As a player I possessed one of the best shots in the game, and I was one of the fastest players ever to have played. I played in two leagues, and the money paid me to leave one league for the other made me the highest paid player in the history of my sport. Because I was

so upset with the unnecessary violence in my sport, I sat out one game in protest of this violence. Everybody supported my protest, but the violence continues. I am one of the greatest scorers in the history of my sport. Who am I?

29) I have won more championships in my sport than any other player in history. Many consider me the finest all around player in history, and almost all agree that no player has the smooth, effortless grace that I have in performing the techniques of our sport. But of all my championships, the one considered by my profession to be the most important, has eluded my grasp—even though I have had a a number of excellent chances to win. I am in my sports' Hall of Fame, and I'm still one of the most popular players with the fans whenever I play. Who am I?

30) Experts in my sport do not know whether I'm the greatest to have ever player or not, but I'm always listed in the top five. In my sport, there are four tournaments that are played each year that make up what we players call the "Grand Slam". I am the only player in history to have won the Grand Slam twice. (Few have won it once.) I have great quickness and speed of foot. Although not as powerful as I was when younger, I am still a contending force whenever I play. Who am I?

31) Although I never played college football, I was drafted by a professional football team when I graduated from college. I was also drafted by a professional basketball team. I tried out for the football team as a wide receiver even though, in high school, I was an All-State quarterback. In college I played basketball, only. I was a member of one of college basketball's greatest teams but one of my teammates far overshadowed me. In the NBA, however, even though he was also a great player with the

pros, I became one of the most respected players in NBA history and one of its greatest performers. I have played on a number of NBA championship teams; and when I retired, all the cities in the league had a special "night" for me when I played my last game in their arenas. Although I could not handle the ball like Cousy, rebound like Russell or shoot like Sharman, many consider me the best all-round player in the history of the NBA. Who am I?

32) I was a member of the United States Olympic team in 1952, the first time the Russians competed. And the man I had to beat in my specialty was a Russian that held the world record. He was the one man the Russians were sure would win a gold medal; and since our event was not a regular part of American track & field, they expected little competition from me. I was working for the F.B.I. then and was granted a few weeks leave to train and go over Finland. Also, I had only run this event about eight times in my life. But I ran the steeplechase and won the gold medal. All America celebrated my victory over the Russian although most Americans had no idea of what a stepplechase run involved. Who am I?

33) I am a five-time champion of my division in boxing. I also held the title in another division for five years. Among the modern day fighters, I am considered to have been one of the best "pound-for-pound" fighters to have ever lived. I made and spent over a million dollars, and at one time traveled with a retinue of thirty people, including my own barber. In one of my most memorable fights, I was badly cut over the eye, and the referee was going to stop the fight when I knocked out my opponent with a left hook that is considered one of the classic knockout punches in boxing history. That knockout enabled me to regain my title. Who am I?

34) In 1968, I was supposed to win a number of Gold Medals for the United States in the Olympic Games. But I was a failure—only winning two golds as part of one of our relay teams. But in 1972, at Munich, West Germany, I astounded the sports world by winning seven gold medals, both individually and in the relays and setting world records in all the individual events. My feat is considered to have matched or exceeded Jesse Owens' achievements in the 1936 Olympics in Berlin. Who Am I?

35) I was Rookie of the Year in the National League, and I have won three Cy Young awards as the best pitcher. I have also led the league with the lowest earned run average three times. I am primarily a fast-ball pitcher and share with two others the record for most strikeouts in a game. But I hold the record for the most consecutive strikeouts in a game. I have played in two World Series, am always on the National League All Star team, and a few years ago when I was traded, the controversy eventually led to the dismissal of my former boss. Who am I?

36) I was the first player chosen by a new professional football league, and I played on championship teams every year in that new league until we joined the National Football League. I was an All America tailback in college and All-America forward in basketball. Also, I was a trumpet player of some talent and and once played with the college band at halftime in my football uniform. I also played pro basketball in the NBA. I am in the pro football Hall of Fame. I led my team to three NFL titles as a player. Who am I?

37) Big time college basketball was played mostly in the east when I was in college. But I came to Madison Square Garden in New York with my teammates to show them that we also played the

game in the west. But it was a different game. We played Long Island University, considered to be the best team in the country, and ran them off the court. The coaches, players and writers that saw me play said they had never seen such an exhibition of shooting. My one-handed running shot brought in a whole new era of basketball, and our fast-break offense brought a new dimension to the game. I never played professional basketball because it was not played in the west then. I am in the basketball Hall of Fame. Who am I?

38) When I came up to the major leagues, I was considered to be a good field-fair hit ballplayer. Over the years, I became the first player in my league to win back-to-back Most Valuable Player awards. I am one of only a dozen or so players to have hit over 500 home runs in their major league careers. I was probably the most popular player to have ever played for the team with whom I spent my whole major league career. I also hold the major league record for home runs hit in one season for players that played the same position I did. Who am I?

39) When I came out of college, I was a number one draft choice in the NFL. I had been an All-America lineman in college. In the pros, I've played both guard and tackle. Many experts consider me to have been one of the best blocking linemen in history, and I have been named to a number of All-Time All-Pro teams. I was inducted into the Pro Football Hall of Fame after I retired. I played head-to-head against another Hall of Famer in the famous "greatest game ever played"—the Colts-Giants NFL title game in 1958. (I was on the winning side.) Who am I?

40) I was never the most popular player when I first joined the pro golf tour; however, I was a win-

ner. The prize money was about a tenth of what it is today, so we had to play almost every week to make a living. I missed one year when I was recuperating from an accident. The next year when I returned, the galleries were really pulling for me. When I played in Scotland for the British Open, the locals called me "the Wee Iceman." Many consider me the greatest golfer of all time, and I have won the United States Open championship four times. Who am I?

41) In 1968 I won the United States Open Tennis championship at Forest Hills and the U.S. Lawn Tennis Association that same year. But it wasn't until 1975 that I achieved my greatest tennis victory. After the success of 1968, I continued to win a number of tournaments but never won any of the major tournaments. But in 1975, I became the champion of what is the most prestigious tennis tournament in my sport. I beat Jimmy Connors for the Wimbelton tennis championship. None of the experts gave me a chance to win the championship, and when I played Connors in the finals, the odds on my winning were very high. Who am I?

42) I am one of ten players named to the Diamond Anniversary All-Time NBA All Star team. I came from a small college in North Carolina, but I never made any of the college All-America teams. The pro team that drafted me had the best pair of guards in basketball, and few gave me a chance to make the team. But I played for over ten years in the NBA and played on a number of championship teams. I am best remembered for my bank-jump shot and the speed with which I would get down court. Who am I?

43) I was a high school running star who came from the same state that gave America its most famous long distance runner in the 1930s. As a college runner, I set the world's record for my spe-

cialty, a record that stood until 1975. Although I was considered the best in my specialty, my Olympic career was a failure in that I never won the gold medal. In the 1972 games, I was the victim of a spill in the qualifying heat and never made it to the finals. But Roger Bannister considers me one of the greatest runners of all time. Who am I?

44) I was the subject of many jokes when I was a fighter, but anyone that fought me knew that he had been in a battle. I was accused of being one of the dirtiest fighters of all time, but I always claimed it was my style that made me look bad. I was short and heavy, and sometimes I'd drink a case of beer after a hard training session. I once knocked Joe Louis down in a championship fight. After my boxing days, I wrestled. And one time I fought an octopus. Who am I?

45) I am the only female athlete to have won the Associated Press Female Athlete of the Year Award for my skills in two sports. I was also named the greatest female athlete in the history of sports. I played baseball and basketball and was a three Gold Medal winner in the Olympics. But it was as a golfer that I gained my greatest fame, and because of me and the publicity I could bring to the women's tour, womens' golf was able to stay alive to reach today's popularity. Who am I?

46) I signed to play major league baseball for a bonus of $100 and a salary of $300 a month. I played 21 years for the same team, and most of the time we finished near last place. But I won over 400 games as a pitcher and set strike out records that only today are being broken. I still hold the record for the most shutouts. When the Baseball Hall of Fame was begun, I was one of five immortals to be inducted that first year. Who am I?

47) I was a 17th round draft choice in 1956 for the team that finally selected me to try to make it in the NFL. Before I retired in 1972, I had won more championships that any other quarterback in the history of pro football. The first year I was eligible to be inducted into the Hall of Fame, I was. I hold the record for having the longest string of passes thrown without an interception and also have the highest lifetime percentage of completions in pro football history for a career. In the games I played, including regular season as well as playoff and championship games, I am "the winningest quarterback" in history. Who am I?

48) At a banquet honoring him as "Golfer of the Year", Arnold Palmer told the assemblage that if it had not been for me, "professional golfers would still be getting their meals in the kitchen." Because of my golfing ability and flamboyant personality, I gave pro golfers their first real acceptance to the golfing public and the sporting press. Until my time, amateur golfers got the big headlines. Five times I won the PGA title, also 2 U.S. Open championships and numerous other national titles. I also beat Bobby Jones in a head-to-head 72 hold match play affair for the "unofficial" national championship. A famous scotch is my name. Who am I?

49) I have won seven American League batting championships and still have a shot at Ty Cobb's record of 12 titles. Although not considered a power hitter, I do manage to get my share of home runs and have the highest season batting average since Ted Williams hit .406 in 1941. I have been voted the Most Valuable Player one season, and in 1977 had the best chance of any player to reach that magic .400 mark. I missed, but I'm young enough to have a shot at it. Who am I?

50) When in college, I was more famous as a blocker for my All-America teammate. But in the pros, I became one of the top rushers in the game. I have always been at my best in the playoffs and hold the record for most yardage gained by any runner in playoff history. I hold the record for the most yards gained in one game in the Super Bowl series. I am also famous for catching a pass that has since been named as the "Immaculate Reception". Who am I?

Answers

1) Bob Feller. He pitched three no-hit games in his career and was considered the greatest strike-out pitcher since Walter Johnson. Feller also had a great curve ball and many batters claimed this was even better than his fast ball.

2) Danny Fortman. He played at Colgate and then with the Chicago Bears. He was an important part of the Bears' famed "Monsters of the Midway" and the team that beat the Washington Redskins 73-0 in the greatest rout in NFL championship history.

3) Abe Saperstein. He started the fabulous Harlem Globetrotters; and because of their popularity, pro basketball teams in the '30s and '40s asked Saperstein to schedule his Globetrotters into their arenas so the fans would come to watch Abe's team and hopefully stick around and watch the pros. It also made a good payday for the pros.

4) Maurice Richard. In the '40s and '50s, the Rocket was the greatest player in hockey and easily the most exciting and controversial. The hockey commissioner suspended Richard just before the start of the Stanley Cup playoffs in which the Montreal Canadians were favored. The city erupted when the suspension was announced, but it stood.

5) Sleepy Jim Crowley. He was one of the Four Horseman of Knute Rockne's great Notre Dame team. He coached Vince Lombardi at Fordham where Crowley's teams were national powers. Lombardi was a guard on Crowley's famed Seven Blocks of Granite team.

6) Stan Musial. His minor league manager, Dick Kerr and his wife, took in young Musial and his wife when Stan hurt his throwing arm. He went on to be one of the greatest hitters in baseball history.

7) Harrison Dillard. He held the world's records in 1948 in the hurdles but lost out in the Olympic trials that year and didn't make the three finalists in any of the hurdle events. Then he made the third place spot on the 100-meter dash team. In Helsinki, Finland, he won the gold medal in the 100 meter.

8) Bob Pettit. He was so bad a player in grammar school and his first two years in high school that he failed to make the junior varsity. His play against the Boston Celtics in the NBA finals in 1957 is still considered one of basketball's greatest playoff performances.

9) Ken Venturi. He had to take salt tablets and have his legs massaged just to make it around those last 36 holes and win the U.S. Open.

10) Tony Zale. His three fights with Rocky Graziano are still considered the greatest trio of championship fights ever fought.

11) Yogi Berra.

12) Bob Cousy. When he came into the league he had been a great college player at Holy Cross and very popular with the Boston fans. When the press asked Red Auerbach if he was going to draft the local hero, Auerbach replied, "What am I supposed to do; win games or play some local hot-shot?"

13) Frank Laehy He coached four Heisman at Notre Dame; Angelo Bertelli, Johnny Lujack, Leon Hart and John Lattner.

14) Warren Spahn. He pitched the Boston Braves into a World Series against Cleveland and then the Milwaukee Braves against the New York Yankees.

15) Bill Toomey.

16) Joe Louis.

17) Glenn Davis. He was "Mr. Outside" to Doc Blanchard's "Mr. Inside" on the great Army teams in the '40s.

18) Ed "Strangler" Lewis. The grip he developed in wrestling is called the "headlock", and he won the title in 1920 with that grip.

19) Jack Kramer. Because of him, the tennis stars of today make the terrific money they do. His tour with Bobby Riggs and later with Pancho Gonzales established professional tennis as a 'big-time' sport.

20) Pele. He came out of retirement to play soccer in the United States; and because of him, pro soccer has a chance of making it in this country.

21) Jerry Lucas. He led the Ohio State Buckeyes to three Big Ten titles and an NCAA championship. In college and in the NBA, he was a great all-around player, rebounder, shooter and passer.

22) Leo Durocher. He was called "Leo the Lip" by his Yankee teammates, because he showed little respect for Babe Ruth and Lou Gehrig and the other Yankee greats.

23) Paul Hornung. The "Golden Boy" played on a Notre Dame team that won 2 games and lost 8 in 1956. He was the bonus choice of the Green Bay Packers; and when Vince Lombardi took over the Packers, Hornung and the team went on to greatness.

24) George Mikan. His coach at DePaul University made Mikan skip rope and jump over chairs to develop coordination. He was the first of the 'big' men in college ball and became the first super star in the NBA.

25) Steve Cauthen. He was the Triple Crown winning jockey aboard Affirmed in 1978 and 1977 Associated Press Male Athlete of the year. And he did all of this before he reached the age of 20.

26) Roy Campanella. The great catcher of the Brooklyn Dodgers won the National League MVP award in 1951, '53, and '55. Only Stan Musial has

been a three-time winner with Campy in the National League.

27) George Blanda. He holds the record for most games played, most years in the NFL, and most points scored.

28) Bobby Hull. He played for the Chicago Blackhawks in the NHL and jumped to the WHL to play for the Winnipeg Jets. In 1977 he sat out a game to protest the violence in hockey. He retired in 1978 having scored over 1000 goals in his career,

30) Rod Laver. He is the only tennis player to have won tennis's Grand Slam twice, in 1962 and 1969.

31) John Havlicek. He had been an All-State football player in Ohio but played only basketball at Ohio State. His teammate was Jerry Lucas, and Havlicek was better known for his defensive abilities. The pro football team that drafted him was the Cleveland Browns.

32) Horace Ashenfelter. Back in 1952, the stepplechase was an event in track and field that few Americans ever saw. Ashenfelter's feat made him an American Olympic 'folk' hero.

33) Sugar Ray Robinson. He won the middleweight title from Jake LaMotta in Chicago in 1951; lost it to Randy Turpin; beat Turpin, in the fight that Robinson's left hook won for him; retired; came out of retirement to take back his title from "Bobo" Olson; lost it to Gene Fullmer; beat Fullmer for it back; lost to Carmine Basillio; then beat Basillio in the rematch.

34) Mark Spitz. He won seven Gold Medals for swimming in Munich in 1972.

35) Tom Seaver.

36) Otto Graham. He was drafted by the Cleveland Browns for the All America Football Confer-

ence while he was in service during World War II. His coach, Paul Brown, built his whole team around Graham, winning all four AAFC titles during the four year existence of that league. They came into the NFL in 1950, winning the title their first year and Graham won another in 1954 and '55.

37) Hank Luisetti. When he came to play against LIU with his Stanford teammates, basketball was a game of set shots, lots of pattern plays, and low scores. Luisetti and Stanford showed the east another game and his running one-hander and the Stanford fast-break opened up basketball to the game as we know it today.

38) Ernie Banks. His great home-run-hitting ability was never enough to carry his Chicago Cubs to a National League pennant, but he is the most popular player to have ever played for the Chicago Cubs.

39) Jim Parker. He came into the NFL and played for the Baltimore Colts. In that great title game, Parker did a fantastic job blocking the Giants' Andy Robestelli, a Hall of Famer himself.

40) Ben Hogan. After his car accident, the public made Hogan their favorite golfer.

41) Arthur Ashe.

42) Sam Jones. He played with the Boston Celtics.

43) Jim Ryun. The state is Kansas, and it gave America Glenn Cunningham, our greatest miler in the 1930s.

44) Tony Galento.

45) Babe Didrikson Zaharias.

46) Walter Johnson. He played his whole career with the Washington Senators and finally played in a World Series against the New York Giants near the end of his great playing days.

47) Bart Starr. He quarterbacked the Green Bay Packers to six Western conference titles, five National Football championships, and victory in the first two Super Bowls.

48) Walter Hagen.

49) Rod Carew.

50) Franco Harris. The back he blocked for at Penn State was Lydell Mitchell, another top pro football player.

Chapter 11
Golf, Tennis, Horse Racing and Other Sports

Two horse racing fans were overheard talking at the paddock at Belmont Race Track in New York one day. They were obviously part of that group that loves racing for the sport and considers itself as "improvers of the breed."

"Look at the beauty of his forelock, the carriage of his head, how the shoulders are so powerfully muscled," one fan said to the other.

"You're right," the other replied. "Your horse is a real beauty. What is his name?"

"Number 6," the other replied.

Racing is indeed a sport of beauty and pagentry and excitement and tradition. It is also the highest attended spectator sport in the world. One wonders how high that attendance would be if all those spectators were there just to enjoy the spectacle and not bet. But once every year, sports fans and non sport fans follow racing because of the Kentucky Derby.

The tradition and pagentry of the Derby are such that every person, fan or not, enjoys Derby Day.

What the Kentucky Derby means to horse racing, so the Masters means the same to golf and Wimbledon to tennis. There are a number of sports that capture the public's attention for a few days, and the winners of the major events in these sports are remembered by the fans. And every four years, the Olympics come on the scene and for two weeks, Americans follow their countrymen as they compete against the athletes of other countries. Sports immortality can come to a gold medal winner if his or her feat captures the imagination of the public. And, fortune can also come to these Olympic amateurs of ours after their Gold Medal days are over. Television or the movies can make them even more famous.

So here are a few questions about heroes and records from the world of sports that do not dominate our sports pages like football, basketball and baseball. In other parts of this book, questions about these sports of tennis, golf, boxing, horse racing and track and field, etc. were asked. But those dealt with athletes and events that any sports fan would be familiar with. These will be a little more difficult, but not too tough.

1. Who holds the record for shooting the lowest 18-hole score in a competitive golf tournament, what was his 18-hole total, in what tournament did he shoot his record low, and in what year?

2. Name the player, besides Bjorn Borg who has won the men's singles at Wimbledon four times?

3. The most important golf tournament in the world is the United States Open Championship. Winning this tournament means more to the golfer

than any other title, both for prestige and money. The tournament was not played during World War II. Since then, name the player that has won the U.S. Open the most times and the number of victories he scored.

4. Name the race horse that is the all-time leading money winner.

5. In the minds of most sports fans, Man o' War is the greatest horse that ever lived. He won 20 of 21 races before being retired to stud. Name the only horse that ever beat Man o' War, where it happened, and in what stakes event, and what year?

6. Only two men ever retired as undefeated heavyweight champion of the world in boxing. Who are they?

7. In the long history of the modern Olympic games (meaning since they were begun back in 1896), what athlete holds the record for the most medals won, including gold, silver and bronze?

8. What was the name of the track star that had his name entered in the record books the most times in one day's competition? Can you give the track meet where this happened and the year?

9. Three of the great barriers in track and field that experts said "could never be broken" were (a) the four-minute mile, (b) the 15-foot pole vault, and (c) the 7-foot high jump. All of those barriers have been broken many times. Name the three track and field immortals that broke those barriers first.

10. In marathon swimming, the most famous challenge is swimming the English Channel. Name the first woman to swim the English Channel and the first woman to swim it both ways.

11. Although amateur athletes seldom capitalize on their fame after their careers, two famous swimmers became movie stars. Both were Olympic gold

medal winners. Name them and the movie role that is most often identified with them.

12. Winning at Wimbledon, especially the singles title is the dream of every tennis player. Name the woman that has won the most Wimbledon singles title and how many times she won it.

13. In auto racing, the most famous individual race is the Indianapolis 500 and the most glamorous races are the International Grand Prix circuit. The World's Driving Championship is based on the Grand Prix circuit. Name the Americans that have been named World Driving Champion. The award began in 1950.

14. Since 1950, name the drivers that have won both the Indianapolis 500 and the World's Driving Championship.

15. Only one driver has ever won both the Indy 500 and the Grand Prix World driving championship in one year. Name that driver and the year he accomplished the feat.

16. In hockey, the trophy signifying the Most Valuable Player is the Hart Trophy. They began naming an MVP back in 1924, and many great players have received the honor. Name the player that has won the MVP the most times and how many.

17. The most difficult position to play in hockey is goalkeeper. The trophy awarded to the hockey player judged to be the best goalkeeper each year is named the Vezina Trophy. Name the goalie that has won the Vezina Trophy the most times in succession, and, if possible, the years he did so and the team he played with while winning the trophy.

18. Only one boxer in history ever held the heavyweight, light-heavyweight and middleweight titles at different times during his career. Who is he?

Hint: his career spanned the late 19th century and early 20th century.

19. In golf, greatness is usually associated with the golfers who win major tournaments, like the Masters, U.S. Open, British Open and the P.G.A. Back in the 20s, the U.S. Amateur was more important than the P.G.A. title. Name the golfer who has won the most "major" golf titles in his career, how many and the golfer who ranks second—counting U.S. Amateur titles from the '20s.

20. Bowling is one our most popular recreational sports. Professional bowling has become a very lucrative business. Name the man that has been named "Bowler of the Year" by the Associated Press the most times, how many times, and the bowler that is the all-time money winner.

Answers

1. Al Geiberger shot an incredible 59 in the second round of the Danny Thomas Memphis Open in 1977. It was the greatest 18-hole round ever played.

2. Rod Laver. He won back-to-back Wimbledon titles in 1961 and '62 and in 1968 and '69.

3. Ben Hogan has won the U.S. Open four times since 1946. He won in 1948, 1950, 1951 and 1953. He lost in a playoff to Jack Fleck in 1955.

4. Kelso. This great horse won $1,977,896. The second leading money winner is Forego.

5. Man O'War's only defeat came at the Stanford Memorial Stakes at Saratoga in 1919. Appropriately, the horse that defeated him was named Upset.

6. Gene Tunney, after defeating Jack Dempsey, held the title from 1926 until 1928; and Rocky Marciano, who won the title from Jersey Joe Walcott in 1952 and retired undefeated in 1956.

7. The Flying Finn, Paavo Nurmi (Finland) won 12 medals in the Olympics. He won nine gold and three silver in competition in the 1920, 1924, and 1928 games.

8. In perhaps the greatest performance in track and field history, Jesse Owens set or equaled six records at Ann Arbor, Michigan on May 25, 1935.

9. The first great barrier broken was the pole vault. Cornelius Warmerdam of the United States vaulted 15 ft. 1-1/8 in. in 1940. Dr. Roger Bannister of England broke the "four minute barrier" in 1954 when he ran a 3 minute 59.4 seconds mile at Iffley Road track in Oxford, England. The day was May 6th. The first man to break the 7-foot high jump barrier was John Thomas in 1960. He jumped 7'2" in

the 1960 AAU track and field championships that year.

10. Gertrude Ederle of the United States became the toast of the nation when she became the first woman to successfully swim the English Channel. Later, after the war, Florence Chadwick of California became the first woman to swim the channel both ways.

11. Johnny Weissmuller won five gold medals in the 1924 and 1928 Olympic Games and went on to fame and fortune as the most famous of movie Tarzans. In the 1932 Games, Clarence "Buster" Crabbe won a gold medal. The games were held in Los Angeles and his good looks and gold medal brought him to the attention of Hollywood and he became Flash Gordon to millions of movie goers.

13. Helen Wills Moody of the United States won the women's singles title at Wimbledon eight times.

13. Two Americans have won the Grand Prix Formula 1 World Driving Championship. They are Phil Hill in 1961 and Mario Andretti in 1978.

14. Mario Andretti won at Indy in 1969 and the Grand Prix in 1978. Jim Clark has won two Grand Prixes and also an Indy 500 as has Graham Hill, winning the Grand Prix in 1962 and 1968 and Indy in 1966.

15. Only the great Jim Clark has won both the Indy 500 and the Grand Prix driving championship in the same year. That was in 1965.

16. Gordie Howe, who holds almost every major record in hockey has won the Hart Trophy six times while playing with the Detroit Red Wings.

17. The Vezina Trophy is awarded to the best goal tender and is based on his average of fewest goals allowed. The marvelous goalie of the Montreal

Canadiens, Jacques Plante, won the Vezina Trophy five times in a row from 1956 through 1960. During that period, the Canadiens won four Stanley Cups.

18. Bob Fitzsimmons won the heavyweight title in 1897 when he beat James J. "Gentleman Jim" Corbett—a knockout in the 14th round. He held the title until he lost it to James Jeffries in 1899. Fitzsimmons held the light-heavyweight title from 1903 to 1905, beating George Gardner for the title and losing to Jack O'Brien. This great fighter was the middleweight title holder in 1891, beating "Nonpareil" Jack Dempsey and giving up the title in 1897 to fight Corbett for the heavyweight title.

19. Jack Nicklaus has won 16 major championships. He has 3 U.S. Open titles, 5 Masters, 4 P.G.A. championships, 2 British Opens and 2 U.S. Amateur titles. His closest competitor for major championships is the legendary Bobby Jones who won 13 major titles; 5 U.S. Amateurs, 4 U.S. Opens, 3 British Opens, and 1 British Amateur.

20. Don Carter of St. Louis has been named Bowler of the Year six times and Dick Weber, also of St. Louis, is the all-time leading money winner on the Professional Bowlers' Tour.

A major motion picture was made of his life and many have called him the greatest all around athlete that ever lived. Who is this great athlete?

Chapter 12
Sports Goes to the Movies

With few exceptions, the motion picture industry has had very little box office success with movies that have a sports theme or that are stories about a sports personality. Recently, the success of "Rocky" and the "Bad News Bears" has led Hollywood back into sports movies.

In the past, the sports movie was almost never taken seriously by the movie goer because they were sports fans and knew that Hollywood usually could not duplicate the reality of sports. So watching Jimmy Stewart limp around like Monty Stratton in "The Monty Stratton Story" while being encouraged by June Allyson, the fan knew that any relation between the real Monty Stratton and his story was purely coincidental.

If any sport did lend itself to professional film making, it was boxing. Here, because of excellent camera work and realistic settings, the fan could get some really first-rate film making; and the actors, for the most part, came across as fighters. Also, because boxing lends itself as a sport to the basic conflicts of life and essentially is a "him against me" story, good authors have always been comfortable writing boxing stories. And it is good scripts that make good films. Some of the biggest stars in the movies had some of their biggest hits playing boxers.

But sports that are team sports commonly fail to make a hit because the audiences know that there is no way a Tony Curtis could quarterback a real professional team or that Dane Clark coached the Harlem Globetrotters. And when the real athlete plays himself, the experience almost always is one of embarrassment for the athlete, the audience and the box office take.

One of the reasons for the success of the movie "Heaven Can Wait," was that Warren Beatty actually played quarterback with and against players from the National Football League. The audience recognized the real pros and knew that the action sequences were as realistic as possible with Beatty giving a good simulation of a quarterback. Also, the story was entertaining. That coupled with the reality of having actual NFL stars playing themselves made the picture a success.

Television has made today's sports hero a member of the family. No actor could play Vince Lombardi or Muhammad Ali or O.J. Simpson or Rod Laver. But television has also brought back some of the old classics in the sports movie genre and some of the real bombs that were made in the 1930s and '40s. The late-late movie often shows us a young James Cagney or Errol Flynn or Ronald Reagan playing a football hero or boxer or race car driver overcoming crooks and injury to win and getting the girl in the end no matter what the odds. The following questions about sports and the movies should not be difficult for most sports fans and late-night television watchers. And since most of the "golden-oldies" have played on television, even the young reader should get most of the answers. There are a few toughies but nothing that the movie/tv sports buff can't handle.

1. Everybody knows Pat O'Brien played the lead in "Knute Rockne—All America." What other famous coach did O'Brien portray, and what was the name of the movie?

2. This great movie star made her singing debut in a sports movie. Who is she, and what was the name of the movie? *Hint*: in a later movie she was given a pair of very valuable red shoes.

3. This fine actor got the lead in a great movie about boxing even though he was an unknown at the time. It was a part that many famous leading men in Hollywood wanted. Who is he, what was the title of this famous film, and who was the leading lady? *Hint*: the movie was originally a Broadway hit, and the actor later won an Academy Award in a movie about POWs.

4. One of the real "camp" movies about sports was "Navy Blue and Gold." Name the three stars of that movie in the late '30s. *Hint*: One later became a famous tv doctor

5. Who played Babe Ruth in the "Babe Ruth Story?"

6. Kirk Douglas was an unknow actor until he made "Champion." Name the three leading ladies he "uses" in the movie and the name of the writer on whose short story "Champion" was based.

7. Warren Beatty wrote, directed and starred in the highly successful "Heaven Can Wait." But the

story was based on a movie made in the 1940s. Name that movie. Who played the title role; and who played the part Beatty repeated, and what sport was he involved in?

8. Who played the title role in "Jim Thorpe, All American", and who played his coach, and what was the name of that coach?

9. "Damn Yankees" was a very successful Broadway musical before being made into a motion picture. Two of the Broadway cast recreated their major roles for the movie. Name them and the team that beats out the Yankees.

10. "Gentleman Jim" was a famous boxing movie. Name the star of the movie, and who played John L. Sullivan?

11. Who played Joe Louis in the "Joe Louis Story?"

12. One of the best sports movies was "Follow the Sun." What famous sports personality was the movie about, who played him, and who played his wife?

13. Auto racing has always been a favorite topic for film makers. Can you give the male star in the following films? (A) "The Crowd Roars"; (B) "The Racers"; (C) "Grand Prix"; (D) "For Love of a Lady"; (E) "The Big Wheel".

14. One of the best boxing movies made was the classic "Body and Soul". Name the male and female leads.

15. Basketball has been ignored by movie makers with a few exceptions. A number of years ago, a basketball story centered on the local college hot shot and a young girl. The movie was titled, "Tall Story". Can you give the male lead, and who played the young girl? *Hint:* the girl is a major star now as is her brother and father.

16. This actor twice played the part where he was the son of fathers that wanted him to be a football star for their benefit. Can you name him and the two movies? *Hint:* he starred in his first picture as a tough kid from the streets of Chicago who goes to the electric chair for murder.

17. A charming movie about baseball was "Angels in the Outfield." Name the actor who played the manager of the team and the name of the major league team the actors represented.

18. Horse racing has always provided a great background for movies. One of the best was shot on location where the Racing Hall of Fame is located. Name this movie, and the male and female leads.

19. A lot of pictures have been made about famous athletes with actors playing the part of the sports star. But three famous athletes played themselves in movies about their lives. Who are they, and give the title for each movie.

20. What actor played the fighter in "Battling Bellhop", and what actress played the part of the tough broad with a heart of gold?

Answers

1. Pat O'Brien also played the part of Frank Cavanaugh in "The Iron Major". Cavanaugh coached at Cincinnati, Holy Cross, Dartmouth, Boston College and Fordham. His nickname came from the fact that in World War I, a German artillery shell exploded near him, almost blinding him, inflicting terrible wounds, but he kept at his command and led his men to safety. His coaching record was 145 wins, 48 losses, and 17 ties.

2. Judy Garland made her singing debut in "Pigskin Parade of 1937."

3. William Holden got the lead role in the classic "Golden Boy." His leading lady was Barbara Stanwick. Every major actor from Gable to Tracy wanted the part but Miss Stanwick had seen Holden in the part and convinced the studio to use him. He became a star overnight. The movie he won an Oscar for was "Stalag 17."

4. James Stewart, Robert Young and Maureen O'Sullivan were the stars of "Navy Blue and Gold." Robert Young is tv's Marcus Welby, M.D.

5. William Bendix played the great Babe Ruth.

6. "Champion" launched Kirk Douglas into his great movie career. (He should have won the Academy Award for his performance.) The three lovely ladies he uses in his climb to the top are Ruth Roman, Marilyn Maxwell, and Lola Albright. The writer of the short story was Ring Lardner.

7. "Heaven Can Wait" is based on the movie "Here Comes Mr. Jordan." Mr. Jordan was played by Claude Raines; Robert Montgomery played the athlete, and he was a boxer.

8. Burt Lancaster played Jim Thorpe; and Charles Bickford played his coach, "Pop" Warner.

9. Gwen Verdon played Lola on stage and in the movie and Ray Walton played Mr. Applegate, the devil's messenger. The team that beats out the Yankees is the Washington Senators.

10. Errol Flynn played "Gentleman Jim" Corbett. He won the heavyweight championship when he defeated John L. Sullivan. Sullivan was played by Ward Bond in the movie.

11. Coley Wallace played Joe Louis. Wallace himself was a ranking heavyweight contender as a boxer.

12. "Follow the Sun" was the story of Ben Hogan. He was played by Glenn Ford and his wife, Valerie, was played by Ann Baxter.

13. James Cagney starred in "The Crowd Roars;" Kirk Douglas had the lead in "The Racers;" and James Garner was the hero in "Grand Prix;" while Clark Gable headed the cast in "For Love of a Lady;" and it was Mickey Rooney that was featured in "The Big Wheel."

14. John Garfield, a brilliant actor was the fighter; and his co-star was Lily Palmer.

15. "Tall Story" starred Tony Perkins, and the young girl was Jane Fonda.

16. John Derek played the son to Broderick Crawford in "All the King's Men," and he starred in "Saturday's Hero." The movie he debuted in was "Knock on Any Door" with Humphrey Bogart.

17. Paul Douglas played the manager of the Pittsburgh Pirates in "Angels in the Outfield."

18. The Racing Hall of Fame is in Saratoga, New York. The movie was "Saratoga," and the stars were Clark Gable and Jean Harlow.

19. Two time Olympic Decathlon winner Bob Mathias played himself in "The Bob Mathias Story;" Elroy Hirsh played himself in his movie

biography, "Crazy Legs;" and Jackie Robinson played himself in "The Jackie Robinson Story."

20. The "Battling Bellhop" was Wayne Morris, and the girl with the tough exterior and heart of gold was Bette Davis. Morris became the mostly highly decorated member of the armed forces from the motion picture industry in World War II. He was a navy pilot in the Pacific campaigns.

This player won the Heisman Trophy in 1978 as a junior. Who is he and can you name the other football players who won the Heisman when they were juniors in college?

Chapter 13
Twenty Trivia Toughies

When sports buffs get together, it doesn't take too long before someone asks who in the group can remember some little known incident or fact about a game or a player or team. Soon, each is trying to top the other with his knowledge of sports trivia. More often than not, the trivia questions reflect the basic meaning of the word; inconsequential or insignificant matters.

But to the sports fan, trivia is fun and the more one can stump his friends, the better the fun. Of course, some trivia players ask questions that are really so insignificant that only they know the answers; that's not really trivia. The questions asked here are of and about major sports events that have been seen on television and reported in the press and over radio. Some statistical knowledge will be necessary to answer some of the questions, but most of them will deal with the personalities and the events that made up some great moments in sports history.

1. Every basketball fan knows that the Boston Celtics dynasty in pro basketball began when they drafted and signed Bill Russell. But before they could draft Russell, they had to get draft rights to him. Name the team the Celtics traded with to get the draft rights to Russell, the players the Celtics had to give to that team, what team Russell played with before joining the Celtics after he had finished at San Francisco University, and when this all happened.

2. The greatest rout in National Football League championship game history was the Chicago Bears 73-0 thumping of the Washington Redskins. The Bears scored eleven touchdowns in that game. Only one player scored more than one touchdown. Who was he?

3. A few players have hit two grand slam home runs in a single game. Only one player has done it in the National League. Name him, the team he played for, and when he did it.

4. They have called the NFL title game between the Baltimore Colts and the New York Giants in 1958 the "greatest game ever played." In the third quarter the Giants stopped the Colts on their 3-yard line after the Colts had first and goal. Then the Giants started a drive of their own. In one of the biggest plays in the game, the Giants' quarterback hit his split receiver over the middle on a post pattern, and he ran to the Colts' 25 where he fumbled. Another Giant player picked up the ball and ran to the one yard line where he was tackled. The Giants scored two plays later, kicked the extra point, and trailed the Colts, 14-10. Name the Giants' players that participated in this play: the quarterback, the receiver, the player who picked up the fumble, the player who scored the touchdown, and the player who kicked the extra point.

5. Since 1900 major league baseball players have hit .400 or better only 13 times. There are a number of players that did hit .400 more than once. Name the players that have hit over .400. *Hint:* There are only eight individuals that have hit over .400 at least once in their major league careers since 1900.

6. Name the only person to have ever been honored by being named to the baseball and pro football Halls of Fame.

7. Since 1900 only eight pitchers have pitched perfect games; i.e., not a runner reaches first base under any circumstance. Name these pitchers and, if possible, the year they accomplished that feat.

8. Name the heaviest and lightest of heavyweight champions; the tallest and shortest of heavyweight champions, and the oldest and youngest of heavyweight champions.

9. This famous sports editor of the *Chicago Tribune* was responsible for promoting the All Star baseball game. He also created the College All Star game between a team of college stars and the champions of the NFL. Who was this editor; where and when was the first baseball All Star game played; who won and by what score; and who won the first college football All Star game.

10. Give the most points ever scored in a college football game, the teams that played and the coach of the winning team. Also, more than that victory, for what is this coach more famous?

11. In question 7, you were asked to name the pitchers that have pitched perfect games since 1900. Of the eight named, one pitcher faced only 26 batters yet he was given credit for a perfect game. Describe the circumstances and the players and teams involved.

12. The record for the most touchdown passes thrown by a passer in a single NFL game is held by a number of players. Name the players that have tied that record, how many touchdown passes completed, and which player set the record first.

13. For hockey buffs, name the fastest skater in NFL history, the most penalized player, the player that holds the season record for most assists, and the origin of the Stanley Cup.

14. Name the Triple Crown winners in horse racing and the name of the horse that was the only undefeated winner of the Triple Crown. How many jockeys have ridden more than one Triple Crown winner and name them.

15. Five heavyweight champions were also gold medal winners in Olympic boxing. Name them. Give the weight class they fought in to win their gold medals and the Olympic year each was a gold medal winner.

16. The term "Grand Slam" can be applied to more than bridge. In sports it can deal with a number of things. Give three sports where the term is used and the term's meaning for each sport.

17. Since 1930 only two men, one from each league, have batted .400 or over. Name them. Then give the exact batting average (and the year each hit over .400). Give the name and the batting average of the player(s) that have had the best batting average in one season in each league since.

18. One of the hallmarks of greatness in an athlete is consistency over a long period of time. The super star for one season who cannot maintain his performance over a period of years seldom makes his sport's Hall of Fame. Three great baseball players played for over four decades. Name them and give the years they played major league baseball.

19. One of the greatest pro football games ever played was the famous "Ice Bowl" NFL title game where the Green Bay Packers beat the Dallas Cowboys 21-17 in a game played on a frozen field in minus 20 degree weather. The win gave the Packers an unprecedented three NFL titles in a row. Jerry Kramer's block that led Bart Starr into the end zone had been very well publicized. Can you name the other Packer player that also threw a key block with Kramer and against whom on the Dallas Cowboys they threw that block?

20. Since 1900 only one team in all of baseball has played an entire season without being shutout. Name that team and the year they were not shutout.

Answers

1. Red Auerbach, coach and general manager of the Boston Celtics knew that if his flashy, high scoring Celtics were ever to win the NBA title, they had to have a great rebounder. Bill Russell, dominating college basketball at San Francisco University, was the player Auerbach wanted. But he knew that he'd never get a shot at drafting Russell because the Celtics were too good and would draft too late to get the great player. The Rochester Royals had the number one choice, but Auerbach knew that the Royals could not afford Russell's expected asking price. The team that would draft second was the St. Louis Hawks. Auerbach offered his star center, "Easy" Ed Macauley, himself the greatest player in the history of St. Louis University, to the Hawks. Ben Kerner, the owner of the Hawks sensed Auerbach's heat to have Russell, so he held out for another player. Auerbach added Cliff Hagen to the pot, and the deal was made. Before joining the Celtics, Russell was on the 1956 United States Olympic basketball team and helped that team to the gold medal before coming to Boston. It happened in 1956.

2. Harry Clark, a running back, scored two touchdowns in that 1940 NFL title game.

3. The only National Leaguer to hit two grand slam home runs in a single game is Tony Cloninger of the Atlanta Braves on July 3, 1966. Cloninger was a pitcher.

4. The quarterback for the Giants in that famous game was Charley Connerly; his receiver was the great Kyle Rote. Rote caught the pass and when tackled, fumbled; and Alex Webster, the Giants' halfback, picked up the loose ball and ran to the Colts' one yard line where he was tackled. Two plays

later, Mel Triplet, the Giants' fullback, scored; and the extra point was kicked by Pat Summeral.

5. Rogers Hornsby and Ty Cobb each hit over .400 three times. George Sisler did it twice. The others are Larry Lajoie, "Shoeless" Joe Jackson, Harry Heilmann, Bill Terry and Ted Williams.

6. Robert "Cal" Hubbard—played football with the Green Bay Packers, the New York Giants, and the Pittsburgh Pirates. In baseball, "Cal" Hubbard was one of the great umpires of all time and was inducted into baseball's Hall of Fame as an umpire.

7. The eight pitchers that have pitched perfect games since 1900 are: Denton T. "Cy" Young, pitching for the Boston Red Sox against the Philadelphia Athletics in 1904, winning 3-0; Adrian C. Joss in 1908 beating the Chicago White Sox 1-0 for the Cleveland Indians; in 1917 Ernest G. Shore pitched the Boston Red Sox to a 4-0 win over the Washington Senators; C.C. Robertson of the Chicago White Sox beat the Detroit Tigers 2-0 in 1922; in 1956, in the only time in World Series history, Don Larsen pitched the perfect game, beating the Brooklyn Dodgers 2-0; Jim Bunning of the Philadelphia Phillies beat the New York Mets 6-0 in 1964; in 1965, Sandy Koufax pitched his perfect game against the Chicago Cubs, winning 1-0; and, the last perfect game was pitched by Jim "Catfish" Hunter, in 1968 when the Oakland As beat the Minnesota Twins, 6-0.

8. The heaviest fighter to be called Heavyweight Champion of the world was Primo Carnera, the Italian fighter who was the story behind a great novel, *The Harder They Fall*. The lightest heavyweight titleholder was Robert Fitzsimmons. Carnera weighed 270 pounds, and Fitzsimmons weighed 167 pounds. Carnera was also the tallest at

6 foot 5.4 inches; and the shortest was Tommy Burns at 5 foot 7 inches. The oldest champion was Jersey Joe Walcott at 37 when he was champion, and the youngest was Floyd Paterson who was 21 when he won the title in 1956.

9. Arch Ward was the creative editor of the *Chicago Tribune* sports department. In 1933, in conjunction with the Chicago World's Fair, Ward convinced the presidents of the two major leagues that a game between the greats of the American League and the National League would spark great interest in the fans and help the city of Chicago and its World's Fair. The American League won the first game, 4-2. The first College All-Star game between the collegians and the pro champions was played at Soldiers' Field in Chicago in 1934 and ended 0-0.

10. Georgia Tech beat poor little Cumberland College by the score of 220 to 0. The Georgia Tech coach was John Heisman. The game was played in 1916. Later, in 1935, the Downtown Athletic Club of New York voted to give a trophy each year to the player judged to be the best in college football. They named the trophy after their athletic director, John Heisman, who had passed on the year earlier. The Heisman Trophy is the most prestigious award in football.

11. In the 1917 game between the Boston Red Sox and the Washington Senators, the starting pitcher was not Ernie Shore but Babe Ruth. Ruth walked the first batter and then questioned the umpire's eye-sight as well as his parentage. The umpire thought that Ruth could use some cleaning, so he sent him to the showers. Shore came in and the batter that Ruth had walked tried to steal second when Shore made his first pitch. The runner was thrown out, and Shore went on to retire the remaining 26

batters without any getting to first. He was given credit for a perfect game.

12. The record for most touchdown passes in a single game was set by Sid Luckman of the Chicago Bears against New York in 1943. After that, Adrian Burk in 1954, playing for Philadelphia, threw seven against Washington in 1954. George Blanda did it against the New York Titans in the AFL in 1961, and Y.A. Tittle of the New York Giants did it in 1962 against the Washington Redskins. The last player to do it was Joe Kapp of the Minnesota Vikings who threw seven touchdown passes against the Baltimore Colts in 1969.

13. According to modern tests, Bobby Hull of the Chicago Black Hawks is recorded as being the fastest skater in NHL history. The most penalized player in NHL history is "Terrible" Ted Lindsay of the Detroit Red Wings and the Chicago Black Hawks. He spent 1808 minutes in the penalty box. The player that holds the record for the most assists in a season is the great Bobby Orr. He assisted on 102 goals in the 1970-71 season. The Stanley cup was presented by Governor General Lord Stanley to the winner of the first playoffs in 1893.

14. The Triple Crown winners are: Sir Barton, 1919; Gallant Fox, 1930; Omaha, 1935; War Admiral, 1937; Whirlaway, 1941; Count Fleet, 1943; Assault, 1946; Citation, 1948; Secretariat, 1973; Seattle Slew, 1977; and Affirmed, 1978. Seattle Slew was the only undefeated horse and Eddie Arcaro rode the winners.

15. The five heavyweight champions that were also Olympic gold medal winners are: Floyd Paterson, Muhammad Ali (nee Cassius Clay), Joe Frazier, George Foreman and Leon Spinks. Only Frazier and Foreman won the gold medal as Olym-

pic heavyweight champions. Floyd Paterson won his gold medal as the Olympic middleweight champion, and Leon Spinks and Muhammad Ali, then Cassius Clay, both won their gold medals as light heavyweight champions, Paterson was the first future heavyweight champion to win his gold medal in 1952. Then Ali won his in 1960; Frazier in 1964; Foreman in 1968; and Leon Spinks in 1976.

16. Grand slam is a term used to describe the winning of four of the major tournaments in golf and tennis. The term is also used in baseball when a batter hits a home run with the bases loaded. In tennis, the grand slam includes the following tournaments: Wimbledon, the United States Open, the French Open and the Australian Open. In golf, the grand slam means winning the Masters, the British Open, the United States Open and the P.G.A. (Professional Golf Association) titles in the same year. No golfer has ever accomplished that feat in modern times since the Masters and P.G.A. replaced the British Amateur and U.S. Amateur as part of the grand slam of golf.

17. Bill Terry of the New York Giants hit .401 in 1930. That is the last time a National Leaguer hit over .400. The best batting average in the National League since Terry's .401 was .385 by Arky Vaughn of the Pittsburgh Pirates in 1935. Since 1941 in the American League, when Williams hit .406, only Williams himself with .388 in 1957 and Rod Carew in 1977 who also hit .388 have had the highest single season batting averages since 1941.

18. The four decades are the 1930s, '40s, '50s and '60s. The three players are Early Wynn, Hall of Fame pitcher with the Washington Senators, Cleveland Indians and Chicago White Sox. Wynn played from 1939 until 1962. The second player is the great

Ted Williams who played his whole career from 1939 until 1960 with the Boston Red Sox. The third four-decade player is Mickey Vernon of the Washington Senators who played from 1939 until 1961. Vernon won two AL batting titles.

19. In that great Packer drive against a superb Dallas Cowboys' defense, the Packers scored with only seconds left on the clock and no time-outs. The play was to be a handoff to one of the Packers' running backs, Donny Anderson; but Starr, without telling anyone, kept the ball and followed Jerry Kramer and Ken Bowman as they double-teamed Jethro Pugh of the Cowboys. So Ken Bowman's block had every bit as much importance as did Jerry Kramer's in getting Bart Starr into the end zone.

20. Only the New York Yankees in 1932 have gone a full season since 1900 without suffering a shutout in regular season play.

Chapter 14
Epilog

The old saying "records are made to be broken" is all so true as we have seen. Most of the records that were set will some day be broken. That's the way it is. After all, records are really the reflection of a person or a team that at one time established a standard of excellence that all others try to beat. The chase after a record can turn the whole sports world on its ear and capture the fancy of everyone. And some records are set without any excitement but those mean as much to the individual as any that are featured in *Sports Illustrated*.

And then there are certain records that may never be broken. And maybe, just maybe, they never should be shattered. It is hard to imagine that someday records set by DiMaggio, Williams, Lombardi's Packers, Jack Nichlaus, Mark Spitz and the Boston Celtics or Wooden's UCLA bunch will ever be broken. But they might.

Experts will argue forever what record may be the most memorable in the history of sports, and that question will never be settled. Games change just enough in equipment and technique that the achievements of athletes in one era can never be really duplicated in another. Those "computer championships" or "greatest fights" really can never match what one team or athlete would achieve against another.

But there are certain records that seem to have the ability to stay alive even though the teams or athletes going after them, by modern analysis, should be able to break them. With what the athletes and teams of today have going for them—better nutrition, better training, better medical supervision and repair, the best tools that have ever been made—it would seem that some of the really great records would fall by the wayside. Let's look at some that belong in that "special" category.

When Joe DiMaggio began his fabulous hitting streak in 1941, there was absolutely no excitement. After all, he was one of the premier hitters in baseball, already considered the logical successor to Babe Ruth and looked upon as probably the finest all-around player in baseball and, maybe, in the history of the game. So there was no special reason to see what he was doing day in and day out as something special. But after he had passed the old record of Wee Willie Keeler and then Tris Speaker, the nation was following "Joltin' Joe" like it would Roger Maris in 1961 and Pete Rose in 1978.

To many experts, DiMaggio's record may be the single greatest achievement in baseball history by an individual. When one looks back at baseball as it was played in 1941, the DiMaggio achievement takes on even greater import. First of all, there were no artificial surfaces then. As all fans know, today's surface gives the batter a tremendous edge because a hard-hit grounder will scoot through the infield much faster than a ball hit on grass. Secondly, there were only eight teams in the American League when Joe set his record, and the minor leagues were loaded with top players so that the average level of ability in 1941 was higher than is the rule in today's game. Some will rightly dispute that statement, but one must remember that baseball was really the *only* professional sport; and all the best athletes gravitated towards the game. With only 16 teams in the major leagues, the level of available talent was higher. But, of course, when DiMaggio set his record baseball was "lily-white."

But the fact that makes DiMaggio's record so special was that he, although a high average batter, was primarily a slugger, a feared homerun hitter, whom opposition managers felt relieved if he got only a single or double against them. It would almost be impossible, given the structure of today's game, for any baseball player to combine the power that DiMaggio had with the batting skills needed to set a consecutive streak. Pete Rose came close, and he's one of baseball's greatest hitters; but even Pete would agree that he should never be equated with Joe DiMaggio when it came to combining power with base hits.

Some other baseball records offer the chance that a player will come along and break them. Someday, someone may hit more than 61 home runs in a season and break Roger Maris' record. And even the Ty Cobb record of 12 batting championships could seriously be challenged by Rod Carew, since he has already won seven and is the kind of hitter that will always hit for a high average. Lou Brock's base-stealing record looks safe for a little while—at least his record for most steals in a lifetime. His single season record could fall soon. The artificial turf gives the base runner a great advantage, and it didn't take Brock himself too many years before he broke Maury Wills' single season mark.

But there are a few other baseball records that may never be broken. They may not be as improbable as DiMaggio's hitting streak, but they are legendary. Will any player come along and hit .424 for a season like Rogers Hornsby did in 1924? Quite unlikely, even given the artificial advantage of modern infields. Is there a hitter on the horizon that will someday drive in over 190 runs in a season, as Hack Wilson did? Many baseball experts think Wilson's record belongs up there with DiMaggio's as far as an unbelievable feat of hitting by one player.

With baseball managers willing to pull a starting pitcher as soon as he gets in trouble, today's pitchers will have a difficult time matching the feats of Cy Young, Walter Johnson and the other lengendary pitchers of the past. Young's record 508 wins for a lifetime puts him out of reach; and Johnson's strike-out record of 3508 is another that looks impossible to reach. Today's game features strong relief pitching, and on many major league rosters, the bullpen is every bit as important as the starting pitchers. And any manager that wants to keep managing will go to his bullpen whenever he feels his starter is in trouble. In the old days, a pitcher pitched his way out of trouble, and if he couldn't, he often wound up the loser. So today's pitcher can not get enough opportunity, even with the increased number of games, to pitch himself out of trouble and hope that his teammates will get him back in the ball game. He usually hears his teammates comeback from the radio in the locker room where he's taking his shower.

When Sandy Koufax pitched his fourth no-hitter,

experts said it would be a record that stood for a long time. Nolan Ryan tied the great Koufax in less than a decade, and he's still pitching and probably will set a new standard before he is finished.

As far as team records go, there probably will never be a team that dominates baseball as the Yankees did from the 1920s to the early '60s. But their record of five World Series titles, from 1949 through 1954, was challenged by the Oakland As in the early '70s and is being challenged by today's edition of the men from the Bronx. But baseball will probably never see a team as dominant as the old Yankees.

The free-agent draft makes it possible to "buy" a winner, but the farm system in baseball is almost nonexistent, compared to what it was years ago. Therefore, baseball clubs cannot depend on getting that fresh talent so necessary every year to infuse with the winning veterans to keep a winning edge. Look at the Yankeess—when Ruth left, along came DiMaggio and a whole host of great players. When DiMaggio was ready to leave, Mickey Mantle was already a superstar. And baseball isn't the only game for today's athlete, so those talented youngsters that might have been willing to wait their chance while riding buses in the boondocks of the minor leagues are playing football or basketball in some college and getting ready for the NFL or the NBA.

If the records of some baseball players set in the past seem almost out of reach by players of today and the future, there are only a few records in football and basketball that will probably last through the next decade. The teams and the players in those sports have, like their baseball counterparts, tremendous advantages in training, equipment and coaching that their sports ancestors never had. But with that increase in the level of support material and a higher degree of professionalism in coaching, there has also been a great proliferation of the number of professional teams in football and basketball. The NFL, for almost 50 years has been in a constant state of flux—not with expansion but with survival. Franchises came and went like players in an all night poker game. Peace came in 1950 when the NFL absorbed three teams from the AAFC, begun after World War II. That peace lasted just 10 years, until 1960, when the American Football League began. The new owners wanted a piece of the action. After six years of warfare, the owners decided that paying huge bonuses to football players was a quick way to financial ruin. And television promised lots of loot if they would marry. The shotgun wedding of the two leagues has led to a degree of financial prosperity for pro football that would dumbfound Joe Carr, Jim Thorpe, Tim Mara and the others that started pro football. Even George Halas, who was there when it all began, can't believe the success of pro football.

With the expansion caused by the merger and the addition of two new franchises, the NFL today has 28 teams, with 45 players on each team. Arguments can be based stating the level of play today doesn't meet that of the early '60s simply because the talent is spread out among too many teams. There is some validity to that idea, but it is almost impossible to prove. Nevertheless, the records set in pro football as well as college football, probably will not survive too long. But there are some that have the opportunity to last for a long time.

When Tony Dorsett rushed for over 6000 yards during his great college career at Pittsburgh, he set a rushing standard that probably will last very long before a collegian comes along to top it. He played for four years while setting that record and was free of injuries. So the back who will set a new standard will have to be a starter as a freshman and average over 1500 yards for four seasons. The Dorsett record looks pretty secure.

Jim Brown's pro record of over 12,000 yards probably will stand up against the challenge of O.J. Simpson becase the "Juice" has had a series of injuries and is in the twilight of his memorable career. But Franco Harris of the Pittsburgh Steelers has a real shot at Brown's record. He gets over 1000 yards almost every season, he is young enough, fast and strong, and most important, he plays on a team with many offensive weapons so the defenses can not "key" just on Harris. All Harris must concern himself with is serious injury. If he can avoid that, he'll have a great shot at breaking Jim Brown's record.

The passing records of Fran Tarkenton would fill a record book by itself. He holds almost all of them, from most completions to most yards gained to most touchdowns. But he'd probably trade the lot of them in for one NFL championship. Tarkenton broke most of John Unitas' records, and now that he is retired, others will try to see if they can match or surpass his standards. To break the records Tarkenton finally established the future record holder will have to have great longevity, be free of injury, and play for a strong team. It is the injury part that sets Tarkenton apart from his fellow quarterbacks. Of today's passers, probably Terry Bradshaw has the best chance to get in on Tarkenton's act. He, playing with a top team, is strong and durable, has great receivers, and with the new rules protecting the good Steelers' receivers, Bradshaw should have an easier time than the passers of the past. Also, the new rules on pass-blocking will help. It is almost like giving the offensive linemen a license to hold.

In terms of team records, the only statistic that really counts is the number of championships won. All the other stuff—about first downs, touchdowns, fewest yards allowed, etc.,—is fine for the publicity men when comparing their team to the other team. But fans and players know, statistics mean nothing if you can't say "champion" when the season ends. The team with the most championships is the Green Bay Packers. They have won 11 NFL titles. That record seems fairly safe. But it is also misleading. Three of those 11 titles came in the late '20s and early '30s when there was no playoff system in the NFL. But the Packers do have the record of eight NFL titles since the playoff system began and even that seems safe. Three of those titles came in the pre-World War II era; if you discount those, then the remaining five NFL titles belong to the Packers of Vince Lombardi.

How safe is Lombardi's Packers record of five NFL titles? And also, they won three in a row, something no other team in NFL history has ever been able to accomplish. Lombardi's team won two of those three in a row after the merger of the NFL-AFL. He also won the first two Super Bowls. But victory in the Super Bowl now means "champions of the National Football League." The only team today that has a shot at beating the Packers record is the Pittsburgh Steelers. They have won three NFL titles in the last five years: 1975, 1976 and in 1979. They are still young and strong and are quite similar to the great Packer teams. But repeating two more times in the NFL over the next two years will be a most difficult assignment. If any team can match the Packers, right now, the Steelers seem to have it going and have the best shot. But the odds are still very much against them.

Vince Lombardi

If team championships mean more than individual records in football, the same is true in basketball. Players score at such a rate now that scoring has lost its importance in judging how great a team is. But one individual scoring record in basketball probably will stand up almost as long as Joe DiMaggio's hitting streak. That is Wilt Chamberlain's 100 points against the New York Knicks. There are no players in the game today that can score like Chamberlain, and any player having a shot at that record would have to be playing with teammates who would sacrifice their shots for that individual as Wilt's teammates did for him. Watching the NBA today, one thinks that the words 'passing' and 'feeding' have been ruled out of players' understanding since they seldom seem to execute them.

There are two basketball team records that probably will never be equaled. The UCLA Bruins of John Wooden set a standard of success in college basketball that will never be matched. From 1964 to 1975, the UCLA basketball teams won ten NCAA championships. Of those record ten wins, they won seven NCAA titles in a row. With the intensity of college recruiting today, there is no way one school will be able to get so many "blue-chip" players that they can dominate college basketball as UCLA did under Wooden.

In professional basketball, the same is true. The Boston Celtics from 1957 until 1969, won 11 NBA titles, eight in a row. There is no way any team will ever be able to match that record in pro basketball. Since 1969, no NBA team has been able to repeat just once. And with the expansion and free agent status of the players, a dynasty is almost ruled out. Maybe some team will come along and win two in a row or even make the finals a few times in addition.

But no team in pro sports even ran off the record the Celtics established and probably never will. The ingredients that made the Celtics were so beautifully meshed by "Red" Auerback, their coach and general manager, that the probabilities of that happening again are almost infinite.

Dominating everything was Bill Russell, possibly the "Most Valuable" player to have ever played the game. His defense and rebounding provided the great Bob Cousy with the perfect compliment for his leadership and ball handling. With Cousy and Russell were Bill Sharman, maybe the best "pure" shooter basketball has ever seen and a tough competitor, plus Tommy Heinsohn, fast, aggressive forward with a fine shooting touch and an excellent offensive rebounder. And Auerbach always had a great bench and players like Frank Ramsey and John Havlicek to come off the bench as the "sixth-man" and give the Celtics instant offense. The players of today have changed in attitude from the Celtics days—and basketball is the poorer for it.

There are many other standards in sports that may never be challenged. It is hard to imagine any golfer winning 19 PGA tour events in one season, especially not 11 of them in a row as Byron Nelson did in 1945. There are just too many great golfers today, as anyone can tell reading the list of unknowns that win major PGA events each week now. In tennis, matching Rod Laver's feat of winning two Grand Slams becomes more difficult because tennis, like golf, is attracting so many good, tough young players that even the tops get knocked off weekly. In horse racing, we went 25 years after Citation won the Triple Crown in 1948 before Secretariat came along in 1973 to win the great races. Since then, Seattle Slew and Affirmed did it, and it looks like winning the

Triple Crown will no longer be the exclusive property of a few horses. It reminds one of what has happened in pro football as far as great runners are concerned. The hallmark of a great rusher was to have gained over 1000 yards in a season and in many seasons, no player made that mark. Now, in the NFL, ten or more runners crack that magic barrier every season. Either the defenses are weaker, or we suddenly have bred a new football player.

Speaking of records that may never be broken, the feat of Mark Spitz in the 1972 Olympics will challenge Olympic swimmers for many, many years. Spitz's seven gold medals won in Munich must rank with Jesse Owens and Paavo Nurmi as the greatest feats in Olympic history. And only a fool would say which is the greatest. All of Owens records have been broken by one athlete or another; the same with Nurmi, and someday Spitz will see his shattered. But that makes little difference. No single individual will break them all.

So what is really the greatest record ever set by an individual or a team? Is it DiMaggio's 56 game hitting streak or Hornsby hitting .424 in one season? Is it the Boston Celtics winning and dominating the NBA as no team has dominated a professional sport, or would you vote for Lombardi's Packers winning three NFL titles in a row against unbelievable odds or the Yankees winning five World Series in a row? Was it Jesse Owens in Berlin showing the Third Reich what a superior human being really is; or was it Spitz; or Nurmi; or Roger Bannister breaking the barrier that all said could never be broken? How about a vote for Jack Nicklaus winning more major tournaments than any golfer ever has and ever will; or Ted Williams winning the batting Triple Crown in 1942 after hitting .406 in 1941? How about the Jets beating the Colts in Super Bowl III and scoring the greatest upset in pro football history and bringing parity to the game; or Columbia beating three-year unbeaten Army in 1947?

And setting records is by no means the only thing that captures the hearts of the fans. When the United States hockey team, a bunch of young college kids, took on the heavily favored Russian team for the gold medal in the 1960 Winter Olympic Games, they turned this country on its collective ear, and their victory was one of the great upsets in the history of the Games. And has there ever been a more improbable story than that of the rag-tag New York Mets winning the World Series in 1969? Or how about tiny, SMU, a 28 point underdog, led by Kyle Rote, playing great, undefeated, #1 Notre Dame off its feet in 1949 before finally losing in the last minutes to superior firepower. Every year in sports brings great upsets that finds the whole country cheering for the underdog, applauding their efforts against the odds. It is the spirit, the will to overcome that moves us to pull for the upset.

It really doesn't make any difference who is chosen as having accomplished the greatest feat in sports or who set the record that will never be broken. What does matter is that great athletes play every day and shoot at the standards of excellence set by their peers and predecessors. Records are made to be broken, and the great fun of sports is watching some athlete or team go after that record. Many will never make it, but all that really counts is that they try and in doing so give all sports fans the thrill of watching and rooting, and then talking about it for years to come.

Answers to color photo captions

1. DiMaggio hit safely in 56 consecutive games in 1941. His streak came to an end in Cleveland before the largest crowd of that baseball season. The pitchers that shut him out were Al Smith and Jim Bagby. Indian infielders, Boudreau and Keltner, made three great fielding plays on sure base hits to stop the great slugger.
2. In 1945 the great Byron Nelson won 19 PGA tournaments, eleven in a row.
3. Yes, Steve Cauthen is the youngest jockey to have won the Triple Crown. And he probably is the only jockey that has a chance to break Eddie Arcaro's record of riding two Triple Crown winners.
4. Fred Perry won three Wimbledons in a row in 1934, '35, & '36.

Answers to black and white photo captions

page 6—Bronco Nagurski. He was named All America at Minnesota at both fullback and tackle and also was an All-Pro at both positions. Nagurski was a charter member of the Pro Football Hall of Fame and his greatest days were those he enjoyed with the Chicago Bears.

page 38—George Halas was one of the founders of the National Football League. He is the owner of the Chicago Bears and coached them for 40 years. His nickname is "Papa Bear."

page 58—The first player who played in a Super Bowl game and entered the Hall of Fame was Starr's teammate, the great Jim Taylor, the Packer's rugged fullback. Taylor's second-quarter touchdown gave the Packers all the points they would need to beat Kansas City in Super Bowl I.

page 70—Gino Marchetti, the great defensive end of the Baltimore Colts, is in the Pro Football Hall of Fame and owns one of the most successful food chains in the country, Gino's.

page 106—Bob Cousy played college ball at Holy Cross University and the first team to draft Cousy for the pros was the Tri-City Blackhawks. But that team folded and Cousy's name was put into a hat along with two others. The Celtics pulled Cousy's name.

page 125—George Preston Marshall, was the founder and owner of the Washington Redskins. He came into the NFL when he was awarded a franchise in Boston in 1932. He moved to Washington and named the team the Redskins in 1937. The two rules that Marshall put through were the formation of two conferences in the NFL and a playoff between the conference winners for the league championship. Marshall got that rule passed in 1933, and in 1934 Marshall got the league to agree to allow a passer to throw the ball from anywhere behind the line of scrimmage, not just five yeards back as had been the rule up to then. This opened up the passing game.

page 157—Jim Thorpe. He was most famous for his feats in the Olympics in 1912 and having his medals taken away when it was discovered he had played semi-pro baseball. Later he starred in baseball and was one of the greats of pro football.

page 166—The player is Billy Sims of Oklahoma. The first junior to win the Heisman was Felix "Doc" Blanchard, the great fullback from Army, in 1945. The second junior to win was fabled Doak Walker of Southern Methodist, in 1948. Vic Janowitz beat out Kyle Rote for the trophy in 1950. Thirteen years passed before junior Roger Staubach of Navy won in 1963. In 1974, Archie Griffin of Ohio State won the first of his two Heisman trophies. Sims is the 6th Heisman winner who was a junior.